GOD'S EXTRAORDINARY GIFTS

*Truth, Energy, Rule Over Sin,
and the Fruits of the Spirit*

JENNIFER A. HILL

Copyright © 2021 by Jennifer Anita Hill
Jennifer Hill Production
Jacksonville, FL 32245

All Rights Reserved
Printed in the United States of America

ISBN: 978-0-9891016-2-2
LCCN: 2021912917
ISBN: 978-0-9891016-3-9 E-BOOK

Except where specifically stated otherwise, all biblical scripture is quoted from the New King James Version (NKJV).

Editor's note
The stories in this book reflect the author's recollection of events. Names, details, and circumstances may have been changed to protect the privacy of those mentioned in this publication. This publication is sold with the understanding that the publisher is not engaged in rendering psychological, financial, legal, or other professional services. If expert assistance or counseling is needed, the services of a competent professional should be sought.

Book Cover & Layout: Summer R. Morris
www.SumoDesignStudio.com

Edited by The Editor Garden, LLC, www.editorgarden.com

*This book is dedicated to God, Jesus, the Holy Spirit,
my spiritual leaders, my daughter, Brittany, and my parents,
the late Aaron and Delores Walker Hill.*

GOD'S
EXTRAORDINARY
GIFTS

CONTENTS

GOD'S GIFTS

"'And you shall know the truth, and the truth shall make you free.'"

JOHN 8:32

W
hy are humans on earth? This was a question within me from the early years of my existence. I wanted to know the *truth*. As a little girl, I perceived God to be mean. My youthful understanding was that if I did not get baptized, God would throw me in a fire and let me burn forever. That was my perception of God when I was young. So I got baptized to avoid going to Hell. In thinking God was mean and strict, I felt discouraged to learn more about God and didn't seek God for answers to my life's questions. I sometimes doubted God's existence.

While growing up in my late teens and trying to figure out life, the future was looking bright. My grades were good, and I had a new car, good credit, great friendships, a nice wardrobe, and a good job. I was feeling happy and thinking I had arrived at what life was about: success, money, friendship, and a loving relationship. I met a man in my late teens.

He said he would give me the world. He promised always to be there for me. "I'm not going anywhere," he said. I wanted a prince charming to shower me with affection. Happiness lasted for several months with him.

Then, just like that, things snowballed downward. I was unemployed with lots of debt and felt abandoned. I struggled with illness, my car was repossessed, my bank account overdrawn, and I was isolated from friends. I dropped out of college and had no skills, no degree, no money, and no love. It felt devastating to me. I had a lot of pain, anger, and unforgiveness toward him and myself. I felt a deep sense of emptiness and depression. My heart, trapped in pain, was my new residence.

Years came and went. Surely, I did not come on earth to just suffer. I was not a bad person; I just wanted what everyone else wants, which is success, love, and happiness. These were my beliefs at that time.

The haunting questions resurfaced within me. *Why am I here? Does God really exist? What is the* truth? But this time, I turned to God, seeking answers.

And God answered me.

God is so kind, loving, merciful, and generous. God freed me from depression, anger, and unforgiveness, and He showered me with overwhelming love. My heart was able to forgive and love again. God allowed me to become aware of His truth.

In this book, I will share His truth with you.

Coming up in this book are stories of Christians, who overcame some of their struggles and found the road to living a life experiencing joy, forgiveness, peace, prosperity, and love. In this book, I will show the extraordinary benefits of earnestly pursuing a loving heart turned toward God the Father, the Son, the Holy Spirit, Holy Angels, and all others.

Part One

UNDERSTANDING GOD'S EXTRAORDINARY TRUTH

Chapter One

DADDY LOVES ME!

"And we have known and believed the love that God has for us. God is love, and he who abides in love abides in God, and God in him."

1 JOHN 4:16

"**M**y daddy loves me!" Trina joyfully shouted.

Her mom was pleasantly surprised and baffled to hear those words coming from her daughter's mouth, because Trina did not have a relationship with her father. So, her mom was eager to know what her daughter meant.

Trina explained that she watched one of Mary K. Baxter's videos on YouTube, which talked about her visit to Heaven. The video inspired Trina to praise and worship our Heavenly Father. While doing so, she felt overwhelming love come upon her.

Trina believes she felt God's love, which inspired her to feel that God is always available. God accepts that she is not perfect, but still provides that invitation of His perfect love to her. Trina experiences feeling loved greater than she had imagined it would feel to be loved and protected by her earthly father. She no longer feels the loss of an absent father, but the gain of a loving and protective Heavenly Father, who will be in her life forever and ever and ever.

God's extraordinary love is available for us all. Invite God into your life and experience God's love in extraordinary ways.

RESIST SATAN AND EXPERIENCE GOD'S LOVE

"Therefore submit to God. Resist the devil and he will flee from you."
JAMES 4:7

Joni has recently become a born-again Christian who loves God dearly. She is currently dating a Christian gentleman, Marcus, with the intention to see if they are compatible for marriage. So far, things are going great. Both her and Marcus discuss hiring a Christian coach to help them date without committing sexual sin and to prevent them from rushing into marriage for the sake of having a sexual relationship. It is both their first time dating without committing sexual sins. Things are going well.

One morning, Joni wakes up from a disturbing dream. Then, throughout the day, she is followed by lustful thoughts of her boyfriend. She feels these lustful sensations, very lightly, on the surface of her skin. As soon as she feels the lust coming upon her, very feather-like, she rebukes the lust immediately by changing her thoughts to the Kingdom of God. The lust spirits were waiting for her to take the bait of entertaining the lustful thoughts.

"No!" Joni says. "In the name of my Lord and Savior, Jesus Christ, I rebuke you and the thoughts being sent to me."

A part of her wanted to complain to God about Satan and his demons resurfacing in her. Then, she thought, *Who am I? If Satan tried to tempt*

Jesus, who is perfect, and Job, who was faithful and living righteously, then yes, Satan can try to tempt me and other faithful Christians. Joni continues throughout her day, rebuking and not acknowledging the lustful thoughts, and the lust spirits moved on.

Our loving and extraordinary God provides us with ways to escape our temptations and renounce demons. Those who genuinely turn away from sin and spend time fasting, praying, walking in the fruits of the Spirit, praising God, and renouncing demons in the name of Jesus with the power of the Holy Spirit are able to send demons fleeing. This will soon become effortless to do so, but it requires Christians to spend more than ten minutes a day with God. It is a lifestyle change. Soon, it will become easier to resist temptation.

TIPS FOR CHRISTIANS DATING

- Avoid being alone together in each other's homes.

- Always date in a group-like environment, such as visiting Disney World, volunteering to help others, going to the beach, attending church gatherings, eating at a restaurant, taking pets on walks or outside adventures, spending time at family gatherings, and attending wellness workshops (i.e., financial, health).

- Gradually spend time together. For the first few months, spend two hours twice a week together.

- Maintain pure thoughts and words toward each other and partake in only G-rated behaviors.

- No kissing, cuddling, or massaging each other at any time. Remember the intention, which is dating to evaluate your compatibility (to be equally yoked) to join as husband and wife.

- Keep God first. If you spent four hours interacting with your boyfriend in a week, spend five hours interacting with our Heavenly Father, such as praying, reading the Bible, going to church, doing intercessory prayer, witnessing to others that Jesus is our Lord and Savior.

- Stay connected to your other healthy relationships, such as your family, friends, and support systems.

- Do not commit to marriage before you have seen how your potential spouse reacts to experiencing stress, frustration, anger, and disappointment, as well as how they handle work-related patterns, money matters, cleanliness, eating habits, selfish or unselfish habits, their health, and their temptations. If any of these behaviors are unbalanced, please get counseling before you agree to marriage. Stay away from those who abuse alcohol or drugs, or who are struggling with anger or abuse issues.

INTERCESSORY PRAYER IS AN ACT OF LOVE

"Brethren, my heart's desire and prayer to God for Israel is that they may be saved."
ROMANS 10:1

Earl is a born-again Christian, who formerly practiced new age spirituality. One day, he went to visit his aunt. It had been more than two years since he had last seen her. Some things had changed for Earl. He stopped streaming porn and reading new age books and he now avoids toxic people. Earl is focused on living a life that is pleasing to God.

After returning home from visiting his aunt, something strange happened to Earl while he was sleeping. It felt like someone was choking him and he could barely breathe. An enormous pressure weighed down on his eyes and mouth. He could not move his body, open his eyes, or use his mouth to scream for Jesus. However, what Earl could use was his own will.

Within every fiber of his soul, Earl screamed in his mind, *Jesus, please help me!* He screamed this repetitiously and he broke free. Earl opened his eyes, sat up, and replayed what just happened. Feeling drained and sleepy, he lay down again. He began to feel hands choking him again. When he called on Jesus, the choking stopped.

The next day, the secular song his aunt was listening to during his visit played loudly in his thoughts, until he turned on a gospel song to get rid of it. He had planned to do intercessory prayer for his aunt; however, he unintentionally became distracted, and soon fell asleep in his hammock, every time he was about to pray. When he woke up the final time and opened his eyes, he saw a huge demon, in the form of an ugly and evil-looking spider that was the size of an average house door. The demon left Earl's hammock and crawled out through his open window.

Earl felt violated. He now understood why this was happening to him and realized his mistake. He recollected his visit with his aunt. While he was at her home, she discussed the places she had been traveling around for the last two years. She had visited some of the most beautiful islands and countries. She returned with souvenirs that she proudly displayed throughout her home. But some of them were idolatrous and had demonic roots. She was drawn to the statues of goddesses, bones, skulls, and others, because of their unique look. Before Earl became a born-again Christian, he did not inquire with his aunt or others of their beliefs. To the best of his recollection, his aunt never went to church, as she was very stubborn and did not ever mention God or Jesus Christ. During his visit, while he enjoyed seeing his kind aunt, it became apparent from listening to her speak, observing her souvenirs, and listening to the lyrics of songs she was playing, there were plenty of spirits in her home and they were not the Holy Spirit.

Earl did not go to her house spiritually prepared, as a believer entering into an unbeliever's environment. He had even skipped prayer that day. He went solely as a nephew spending time with his aunt. As he drove away from her home, he thought of ways to start a conversation about Jesus with his aunt. He thought he might start a history project and ask her help, where he could seek opportunities to discuss what Jesus did in Jerusalem, Bethany, Galilee, and is still doing today across the world. He got excited about his ideas, but unbeknown to Earl, he underestimated the spiritual work needed to win her soul to Jesus.

He now realized that those demons probably followed him from her home and were trying to sabotage his plans. They were trying to distract and intimidate Earl from doing intercessory prayer and making plans to win his aunt's soul to Jesus Christ. Earl's prayer plans were to ask God to allow the Holy Angels to remove all demons from around her, so she could receive the words of the Gospel. Earl was going to plant seeds in her mind as he witnessed to her that Jesus Christ loves her. Those demons were trying to disrupt his sleep at night, to frighten him, and keep him too tired and sleepy in the daytime to do intercessory prayer for his aunt.

This battle went on for a few days. Earl went on a fast, without eating for 24 hours. For the following few days, he fasted from all flesh desires (except water). Instead, he prayed, worked, read the Bible, and gave thanksgiving to God.

Those demons stopped fighting him and fled after a few days. Earl became available to pursue winning his aunt's soul to Jesus. Earl has now adopted a lifestyle, which includes the continuation of intercessory prayer for his aunt, without the interruption of demons.

On a brighter note, an old friend named Randy contacted Earl through Facebook. Randy invited Earl and his wife to eat barbecue and watch the game on Saturday. Earl's wife was working and could not attend. However, Earl was available and saw this as an opportunity to witness to Randy's family. Earl had learned after visiting his aunt to always be spiritually prepared to win souls and conquer spiritual battles wherever he goes. Therefore, a week prior to going to Randy's home, Earl prepared to conquer any demonic attacks. He fasted, prayed, and performed intercessory prayer a week prior to going to Randy's home.

At Randy's, they laughed, joked, and discussed old times. Earl started to tell Randy's family that he now feels so much peace and love. Before the family had a chance to assume Earl was gushing about his wife being the source of this love, Earl said, "It is because of my intimate relationship with Jesus Christ."

He continued, "God has opened so many doors for me and removed my urge to watch pornography. The thought of it makes me want to vomit."

Randy just stared at Earl, looking stoned from the liquor he consumed. But Randy's wife, who became teary-eyed, said, "I want a relationship with Jesus Christ."

Earl joyfully discussed salvation and invited them to attend church with him.

When he returned home from Randy's house, Earl resumed fasting and praying. Earl realized that when he pursues winning souls to Christ, he is in a spiritual warfare with Satan. However, Satan is powerless when Earl executes his God-given power through Jesus Christ. He slept peaceful after he returned from Randy's home. Earl has truly established a lifestyle, which includes intercessory prayer for others.

My extended family of sisters, nieces, a daughter, and cousins join once every two weeks and perform intercessory prayer for family and friends. Our loving God gives us intercessory prayer for others. This is a powerful way that believers can send requests to God for healing, breakthroughs, answers, and many other things on behalf of others.

What about you? Who intercedes for you? Who do you intercede for?

BREAK FINANCIAL BONDAGES AND EXPERIENCE GOD'S LOVE

"Therefore keep the words of this covenant, and do them,
that you may prosper in all that you do."
DEUTERONOMY 29:9

Cassie could not catch a break. It was 3:00 a.m. and her neighbor's dogs had finally settled down.

"Maybe now I can get some sleep," she said.

Unfortunately, this was not for long. Her nephew awakened Cassie around 6:00 a.m. because the house's water leak had gotten worse, and things were getting wet. Her landlord had previously cut and pasted the leak and mold issues, which caused the problems to reoccur, and each time, the wetness became worse. She had lost furniture and other items because of the water spreading within her home. The landlord would not compensate for her lost. She wanted badly to move, because it was always one problem after another with the home. Cassie's sister Sabrina, who is a born-again Christian, offered to help her, but with some conditions. Cassie must stop stealing from others because financial hardships followed Cassie wherever she lived.

Sabrina believed Cassie might have a financial curse against her. She believed the attacks might exist because of Cassie's financial sins of cheating the government. She reminded Cassie that falsifying information to the government, to avoid paying what she owes and obtain money she does not qualify for, is unlawful and a sin. Breaking the financial laws of the land, lying, and stealing give demons access within her life to cause havoc.

Sabrina discussed Romans 13:1-7 with Cassie: "Let every soul be subject to the governing authorities. For there is no authority except from God, and the authorities that exist are appointed by God. Therefore whoever resists the authority resists the ordinance of God, and those who resist will bring judgment on themselves. For rulers are not a terror to good works, but to evil. Do you want to be unafraid of the authority? Do what is good, and you will have praise from the same. For he is God's minister to you for good. But if you do evil, be afraid; for he does not bear the sword in vain; for he is God's minister, an avenger to *execute* wrath on him who practices evil. Therefore *you* must be subject, not only because of wrath but also for conscience' sake. For because of this you also pay taxes, for they are God's ministers attending continually to this very thing. Render therefore to all their due: taxes to whom taxes *are due*, customs to whom customs, fear to whom fear, honor to whom honor."

Sabrina proposed to help Cassie if she stopped stealing. Otherwise, Sabrina strongly believed Cassie's hardships would continue to follow her and it would be fruitless to help Cassie move again. If Cassie accepted her proposal, Sabrina would pay for Cassie's moving expenses, her deposit, and the first month's rent. But until then, Sabrina continued to do daily intercessory prayer for her sister.

If the laws of the land do not contradict God's commands, we are to comply with the laws of the land. If they *do* contradict God's commands, do not comply with the laws of the land, and go about the problem gently and with wisdom.

God's prosperity can be manifested and multiplied in Cassie's life. Financial bondage can be broken. True repentance can lead to ending her financial sin, which is stealing. Stealing can be committed in many ways, such as stealing someone's spouse, a job or opportunities, an unrighteous forfeiting of an agreement that causes a loss, falsifying a document to receive a gain, and other similar behaviors. All of these can manifest financial problems.

BE WATCHFUL OF SATAN TRYING TO SEPARATE YOU FROM GOD'S TRUTH

"Be sober, be vigilant; because your adversary the devil walks about like a roaring lion, seeking whom he may devour."

1 PETER 5:8

While waiting to complete the closing process on her new home, Keisha temporarily moved in her cousin's, Bridgett's, apartment. One day, Keisha was sitting in her car and saw a silhouette of a male figure, almost as tall as the ceiling and dressed in a black coat and hood. He moved quickly past their neighbor's living room. It happened so fast, at first, she did not know if it was a person in costume or a ghost. She realized her neighbor, who lives alone, was currently at work.

Keisha hesitantly mentioned it to Bridgett. She had already told Bridgett, the first week she moved into her home, she had dreamed that the community Bridgett and she were living in was surrounded by a lot of snakes (evil-like personalities), and they must be watchful. So she did not want to be the bearer of more bad news. To Keisha's surprise, Bridgett had also seen a dark, ghost-like figure moving around her own apartment. The figure moved and disappeared quickly out of sight. Keisha then felt comfortable to tell Bridgett about her dream from last night. After watching a very wholesome, G-rated show, Keisha had the vilest and most disgusting dream of the two male characters doing R-rated behaviors with each other. As Keisha described the dream she had, Bridgett confessed she also had similar homosexual dreams since she had been living in her apartment.

Bridgett went on to share another weird experience. One day, while Bridgett was at the apartment complex's playground with her dog, she met a young girl who lived in the neighborhood. She was very friendly toward Bridgett's dog. After eating some of Bridgett's snacks and playing with her dog, the adolescent asked Bridgett to become friends with her mom. She provided her mom's name and said they lived on the next block. Bridgett took down her mom's name. She felt confused because she thought the adolescent was a boy until she told Bridgett her name. She also felt a little awkward accepting the invitation, but she shook it off, as perhaps the girl wanted to have a reason to come over and play with her dog.

That night, she attempted to pray for the girl's mother when an evil-sounding, female voice screamed loudly, "Do not say her name! Do not pray for her!" Again, she began to pray, and the voice screamed, "Do not say her name!" Bridgett stopped and decided this prayer would require fasting.

Bridgett and Keisha continued to compare notes about their strange encounters.

Keisha shared that the lyrics from a secular song she heard on the radio more than ten years ago were repeatedly coming into her thoughts. When the old song first resurfaced to her thoughts, it made no sense to her, so she ignored it. But it continued to come. She looked up the meaning of the song and the artist. It was about a woman's love for another woman. The same year the song came out, the artist of the song came out of the closet and confessed to the world she was gay and she was singing about a woman. As Keisha researched photographs of the artist when she first came out, the artist looked like a woman. In more recent photos, she now looked like a man, as her hair was chopped off and she dressed masculine.

The adolescent girl, the elderly neighbor next door, and the single mom across the street all looked, talked, and dressed like men. They had either chopped their hair off or looked masculine. Keisha and Bridgett compared their encounters, and everything started to come together. The vile, gay dreams they had never had before. The silhouette of the demonic figure they both saw, separately and on different occasions. The gay artist's song constantly playing in Keisha's thoughts. The women's appearances changing from feminine to masculine. And, although unrelated, theft in the community was extremely high. They concluded that demons were attacking females with homosexual dreams and thoughts to influence homosexual sins.

So, they prayed and fasted for the community. During one of the prayers, Keisha received a clear thought from the Holy Spirit to write letters to the churches in the community and inform them of the spiritual warfare in the neighborhood. Keisha wrote letters, asking the churches for their prayers and to visit the community. After three months of living in the community, Keisha's new home was completed and ready to move in. Before she moved, a pastor and a church member approached her in the neighborhood with an invitation to their church. Her last three weeks at the apartment, she saw the same pastor and church member return weekly and go door-to-door, inviting residents to church. She even saw them praying with one of her neighbors. Keisha was so happy because she knew God was answering their prayers.

The love God provides us is more powerful than any sin Satan tries to tempt us with. Intercessory prayer is an extraordinary way to help others turn away from Satan and toward God.

Chapter Two

SPIRITUAL WARFARE EXISTS

"For we do not wrestle against flesh and blood, but against principalities, against powers, against the rulers of the darkness of this age, against spiritual hosts of wickedness in the heavenly places."

E P H E S I A N S   6 : 1 2

Early on, before I understood the magnitude of demons and how to defeat them, I experienced what some would describe as vertigo. For me, to best describe what felt like sheer terror, I felt like a strong demon was grabbing me and violently slinging me to Hell and back. My strength rapidly left my body. I felt scared, weak, and lightheaded. I was pleading to God to not let me die. I sat still on my bed for a while, feeling very nauseous. Slowly, I raised myself up and walked around.

I made an appointment with a physician. Many types of tests were performed, and all of the tests came back as normal. However, my balance was still a tad off for a few weeks.

Was this a spiritual attack? I thought.

The next day, when I fell asleep, I was attacked by what some would refer to as "a witch on my back." It happens while sleeping; you are conscious, but you cannot move your body. During the attack, I called to Jesus and I broke from the demon. The following night before I went to sleep, I was lying in bed. Dozing off, I felt something heavy pushing down on my head, as if it were trying to get inside of my head. I was too weak to try and focus on it. It didn't hurt like a headache and I did not see anything on me, but I still felt it. I went to sleep. I awakened again from another attack, where I was conscious but could not move.

That morning, something different happened to me. There was a strong, lustful feeling stemming from within me. I knew then, without a doubt, I was being spiritually attacked. In my heart and mind, I had not desired anyone in more than seven years. I was single at the time and extremely focused on winning souls to the Kingdom of God. My heart and mind were against the lustful feelings that were being sent to my physical body. Now, I was angry. When I returned from work, the lustful urge continued. A part of me was relieved, because I realized it was just a lust demon and not an illness. The other parts of me felt scared, because at that time, I lacked knowledge and experience on how to make these demons flee.

During the first few days, I fearfully prayed for the Holy Spirit to come and make the attacks go away. I searched for information about those who had been delivered from demons. I started watching some of the late Derek Prince videos on being delivered from demons, which currently can be found on YouTube. This led me to ask God to reveal any curses and sins unbeknown to me that were giving demons the legal rights to form against me. I repented and asked for forgiveness for the known and the unknown sins in my life.

I must admit that I was full of fear and only had what felt like *less than* a mustard seed of faith in regard to fighting Satan. This was all new to me. I had been a lukewarm Christian for years and never experienced such attacks. However, the attacks came the week I decided to stop being a fruitless Christian and started investing time into forming an intimate relationship with Jesus Christ and to wins souls to the Kingdom of God.

The attacks while I slept stopped occurring. However, the sexual urge came and went, trying to get a response out of me. God strengthened me to maintain self-control during these attacks. I was not enticed by the urges, but I was aggravated. I prayed throughout the day and most of the night, asking God to continue to give me strength and insight on warding off Satan's demons.

One night, while I was lying in my bed with my head resting on my pillow, I looked up in the air and I saw a young male face looking back at me. I continued to look up at him, while he was looking at me. But it was as if he was looking *through* me, as he did not look into my eyes. He was looking as if he was peeping through a doorway to see what was happening. *What was her next move?*

I realized I was seeing a vision of him, watching me. Needless to say, when the vision of him went away, I immediately got out of bed and started praying and asking for protection while I slept.

When I woke up, I heard a demon speaking, deep down in my ear drum. She came to harass me. The tone of her voice sounded entitled and filled with extreme hatred. She accused me of being sexually immoral. I knew then I was dealing with demons, who had legal access to my body because of my sexual sins in the past. Yes, I committed sexual immorality in the past. However, right before these spiritual attacks, I had recently become sincere about giving my life to Jesus and decided to win other souls to Jesus. I was unaware that I had been housing demons, who were putting up a fight to not give up their residence within my body. In my mind, I thought all was well within me, because it had been more than seven years since I had even desired that sin and I had continued not to lust.

I prayed and read the Bible before I went into work. Driving to work, I received a clear thought from the Holy Spirit, saying, *Fast and pray to cast the demon of sexual immorality out of your body.*

My fear of Satan's attacks began to subside. I began to feel empowered from gaining God's knowledge on fighting this spiritual battle. I pondered about when to start my fast.

The next morning, while awakening from sleep, another attack came upon me, where I was conscious but could not move.

But, this time, it was different. I instinctively tried to turn around and look at what was grabbing me. Simultaneously, I was calling on Jesus' name for Him to rescue me. During this attack, I noticed I felt more empowered. I could make some movement, barely, and I could now see into the spiritual world. There was rapid and strong movement; I saw an image of twirling, strong winds with evil-looking eyes. Although I could not wake fully and get up, I was not afraid.

I felt frustrated and ready for battle. I was not awake enough to process that demons do not have physical bodies, but I instinctively tried to physically fight and grab at what was holding me down. As I tussled, I grabbed my own wrist. I immediately opened my eyes after overpowering the demon.

Feeling empowered through Jesus Christ's strength within me, I knew that no weapons formed against me would prosper. I was more determined than ever to fast. I fasted, prayed, repented, and renounced demons for days. The sexual demons stopped harassing me. The attacks ended.

Along with spreading God's love, fasting, renouncing demons, and praying became a part of my lifestyle. I was then able to focus on winning souls to Christ.

Our loving God provides us with His overwhelming mercy, forgiveness, undeserving grace, and the power to renounce demons. We have legal rights as God's children to rule over sin.

Now, when other demons make attempts on me from time to time, I boldly renounce them in the name of Jesus with the power of the Holy Spirit.

They are all around us. As you learn to self-deliver from demons, your fear leaves and it feels effortless to run them off each time. It becomes as easy as drinking water. Whenever they return, go to battle, annihilate them, and they will flee again. They are no match against the faithful believers who practice loving all. Love covers a multitude of your sins.

Some of the ways to express love is to sincerely and with humility repent to God of your sins. Strive to forgive others daily. Next, strive to express love to all who come within your thoughts or sight, by performing intercessory prayer for them. I pray for my family, friends, employers, neighbors, animals, enemies, and others, believing and hoping in the best for them. Strive to speak gently to everyone you interact with. Forgive those who offend you and give to those who are in need.

PROPHESY DREAMS WARN US OF THIS WAR

"And it shall come to pass in the last days, says God, That I will pour out of My Spirit on all flesh; Your sons and your daughters shall prophesy, Your young men shall see visions, Your old men shall dream dreams."

ACTS 2:17

23

In my dream, I saw a vision of thousands of people walking in rows of long lines, moving farther and farther out in a deserted area. It looked as if they had been traveling on their journey for an awfully long time. Too long. Some of their facial expressions were as if they were carrying heavy weights on their backs and shackles around their feet and hands. Their minds were distracted with what appeared to be worldly interest. They were oblivious that Satan was leading them. They could not see Satan or his demons. They continued walking along the wrong path. Their thoughts were oppressed, believing the lies and ideas that Satan's demons were saying to them. They thought those were their own ideas and thoughts. But all of it came from Satan and his demons. They were filled with deception. The Holy Spirit grievously respects the sinner's will to sin. Actively sinning and rejecting Jesus is what led them further and further into more of Satan's bondages.

My spirit wanted to scream and say, "Hey! Please stop what you are doing! You are going in the wrong direction! It is a prison of more bondages! Turn around!" But they could not hear or see me.

In the same vision, but a different scene, I saw one of Satan's demons watching a Christian. The demon was sending problems her way. The Christian lady was spiritually attuned and realized that things were suddenly difficult throughout her day. Whatever could go wrong went wrong. She misplaced her wallet. The demon was waiting for the Christian to become frustrated and angry, because often a person will sin when they get angry. But, instead, the Christian began to think and concluded that if something was going wrong in the physical world, something was also happening in the spiritual world to shift that change. The Christian concluded that demons were currently around her. She started praying and renouncing them. The demon saw her praying and he began to speak rapidly in the spiritual world to block the Christian's prayer. The Christian prayed with faith and determination. She felt the presence of the Holy Spirit. The demon vanished. She began to praise the Holy Spirit. In one day of becoming aware of her attack, through the Holy Spirit, she defeated what could have escalated to unnecessary and prolonged problems in her life.

But things were not as fortunate for those thousands of people being led further into deception. They did not have the same awareness and recourse to get rid of Satan, because of their active sin and refusal to turn toward God. They were prisoners of Satan, consumed with the oppression and bondages within their life. If only they had the knowledge to understand that through faith in Jesus Christ, they could get out of bondage.

UNDERSTAND YOU HAVE AN ENEMY

"Now the Spirit expressly says that in latter times some will depart from the faith, giving heed to deceiving spirits and doctrines of demons."

1 TIMOTHY 4:1

Demons are commonly known as unclean spirits, familiar spirits, demonic spirits, and evil spirits. Demons are of Satan's evil kingdom. They all have evil powers and different assignments in people's lives. Their assignments are to trick and manipulate people to make choices, which ultimately entrap them in sin enslavement.

Demons do not have physical bodies, but they can legally enter into humans' bodies when there are certain active sins. They are like hateful and evil people, but without bodies.

Faithful Christians are a massive threat to demons. Faithful Christians are believers of Jesus Christ and live a life of love, forgiveness, repentance, prayer, faith, supplication, thanksgiving, and the ability to renounce demons in the name of Jesus with the power of the Holy Spirit.

Demons hate anything that represents righteous love. Demons are empowered through sin. They are not your friends. Satan and his demons hate us. They seek to steal, kill, and destroy the opportunity for souls to live an eternal life with God. Demons study a person's likes and dislikes. A demon's intent is to influence humans to do sinful activities and behaviors, such as sexual immorality, sensuality, idolatry, sorcery, enmity, strife, jealousy, fits of anger, rivalries, dissensions, divisions, envy, drunkenness, orgies, and others like these. The unbelief that Christ is our Lord and Savior, unrepentance, unforgiveness, the refusal to love, and the refusal to turn away from these types of sins are all pathways toward Satan's deceit and enslavement within a person's life. At times, demons communicate to us within our thoughts, visons, sounds, and dreams. Thankfully, our Holy Angels also communicate within our thoughts, visions, sounds, and dreams.

Our comforter, the Holy Spirit, communicates with our reborn spirits. The reborn spirit communicates to our souls through our thoughts, dreams, sounds, and visions, giving edifying information to inspire and warn us. The Holy Spirit comforts us. The Holy Spirit reminds us of Jesus' teachings. The Holy Spirit empowers us to strengthen our will and energy, and to provide the ability for us to walk in the fruits of the Spirit, which move us into a loving atmosphere.

The energy from such a loving lifestyle alone provides us with a lot of strength to control our sinful nature and rule over sin. Always be on guard. When a person willingly chooses to turn toward certain sins, demons have legal rights to send impure thoughts, the energy of negative emotions, and dreams to instigate fear and strife. This creates a pathway to persuade us with more damaging sins. As a person indulges in certain sins, his or her strong energy within and around the physical body can become impaired with holes or cracks, which cause a person to be more susceptible to harm. The energy that covers our body helps to protect us from many things, such as accidents and illness.

For example, say a driver's car crashed, but the driver did not receive even a scratch or a cut. They walked away unharmed. Our extraordinary God gifted our bodies with an invisible covering of energy that I call *body covering*. As we love, this energy replenishes with strength; as we repent, it replenishes; as we forgive, it replenishes. However, certain sins, such as the ones mention earlier, can create holes in our energy, some faster than others. For example, a lie that causes someone to go to prison or to be killed will cause holes in someone's body covering energy much sooner and larger than a lie about cheating on a school test. Try your absolute best not to hurt people or animals, as it impacts the condition of your energy, as well as many other things. Sincerely repent, forgive, and love daily. It can restore the physical and spiritual body consistently.

As a person actively sins, the Holy Spirit will grievously step back and allow a person's will to be done. Then, demons move forward and work through your body covering. The body covering helps to cover, shield, and protect the physical body and mind from harm within the surrounding environment. Just as you would send your child to the beach on a beautiful, hot, sunny day with items that help keep him or her feeling comfortable, safe, and healthy (such as skin protector, swimming attire, sunglasses, fluids to drink, a chaperon, et cetera). Well, God provides plenty of resources for everyone, and energy is one of them that helps aid our physical bodies and minds while on earth. However, certain sins negatively impact the body covering, impairing it with cracks and holes. Demons work hard to enter those holes and cracks in order to enter within the body to instigate more problems in a person's life. They pursue to instigate certain sins, which will harm more of your energy, by creating more holes or tears, working their way throughout the body. The thoughts received from demons will then increase. A person's consciousness dims. An upcoming story of Donald and Janice is an example of how willingly choosing to sin can cause preventable problems.

The great news is that God provides many ways and opportunities for Satan to be powerless within our lives. The power of the Holy Spirit can repair and restore the holes and cracks of a person's body covering, rid demons, and help strengthen your will. Allow your will to be focused on choosing an intimate relationship with God, Jesus Christ, the Holy Spirit, and Holy Angels. Choose to live a fruits-of-the-Spirit lifestyle, which is to abide with the Holy Spirit, walking in *love, joy, peace, patience, kindness, goodness, faithfulness, gentleness*, and *self-control*. The mere intention and effort to walk in the fruits of the Spirit sets in motion for you to experience love, joy, peace, patience, kindness, goodness, faithfulness, gentleness, and self-control.

RENOUNCE DEMONS IN YOUR OWN LIFE

Demons strategize ways to keep people distracted from learning and following Jesus Christ's teaching. They sometimes try to influence you to feel sleepy when you pray or read your Bible. Make sure that love— through prayer, praising the Father, the Son, and the Holy Spirit, reading the Bible, and worshipping—is the first thing you should do each morning and the last thing you should do at night. Demons strategize ways to hinder people from doing the work that has been assigned to them for the Kingdom of God. Demons are aware that everyone has spiritual gifts. They seek to hinder you from using your talent to win souls to Jesus Christ, and instead use it in a way to lure you into enslavement of sin. For example, gifted and talented singers can use their voice to lead a lot of souls to Christ, instead of influencing souls to focus on flesh gratifications.

Who is the influencer behind the songs you listen to? Is it the Holy Spirit or demons?

Below are some tips on how to renounce demons and how to win whatever battle they bring you:

- Pray every day for the Holy Spirit to protect you and bring awareness of any sin of which you may need to repent. Thank God, Jesus Christ, and the Holy Spirit daily.

- Watch Derek Prince's video on YouTube titled, "Turning Curse to Blessing" and Prophet Ugo Ezeji's video titled, "Terminating Demonic Assignments."

- Righteously *love!* Love covers many sins. Demons feed off sin. Love, forgive, and repent every day to help keep the demons away. Be happy.

- From your heart and with faith, call out to Jesus for help when the demons are bothering you. Demons tremble and back off when you call with faith on Jesus Christ.

- Memorize Psalm 91 and speak it with faith:

    "He who dwells in the secret place of the Most High shall abide under the shadow of the Almighty. I will say of the Lord, 'He is my refuge and my fortress; My God, in Him I will trust.'

Surely He shall deliver you from the snare of the fowler And from the perilous pestilence. He shall cover you with His feathers, And under His wings you shall take refuge; His truth shall be your shield and buckler. You shall not be afraid of the terror by night, Nor of the arrow that flies by day, Nor of the pestilence that walks in darkness, Nor of the destruction that lays waste at noonday.

A thousand may fall at your side, And ten thousand at your right hand; But it shall not come near you. Only with your eyes shall you look, And see the reward of the wicked.

Because you have made the Lord, who is my refuge, Even the Most High, your dwelling place, No evil shall befall you, Nor shall any plague come near your dwelling; For He shall give His angels charge over you, To keep you in all your ways. In their hands they shall bear you up, Lest you dash your foot against a stone. You shall tread upon the lion and the cobra, The young lion and the serpent you shall trample underfoot.

'Because he has set his love upon Me, therefore I will deliver him; I will set him on high, because he has known My name. He shall call upon Me, and I will answer him; I will be with him in trouble; I will deliver him and honor him. With long life I will satisfy him, And show him My salvation.'"

- Say thank you daily to our Holy Angels for all that they do to keep us safe. They go to battle for us. They warn us of upcoming challenges. Thank God daily for allowing the Holy Angels to always be armored to protect you. Request the Holy Angels to bring you extra doses of power from the Kingdom of God. Ask the Holy Angels to help bring your prayers into the 3rd Heaven and to our Heavenly Father. Ask the Holy Angels to keep you from harm and to help heal you. Give thanks to the entire Kingdom of God.

Chapter Three

CHOOSE GOD'S LOVE

"Beloved, let us love one another, for love is of God;
and everyone who loves is born of God and knows God."

1 JOHN 4:7

There is one God, who is the Father, the Son, and the Holy Spirit. God's love surrounds us in an abundance of ways. The Father, Jesus Christ the Son, the Holy Spirit, the fruits of the Spirit, the Holy Angels, the faithful saints, the good Samaritans, our free will, and our human energy are all extraordinary blessings available to us. These blessings help us to love, rule over sin, defeat Satan's schemes, and live an everlasting, victorious life. Believers can be prayer warriors, releasing power in the name of Jesus, through faith and prayer. Believers must diligently work hard to stay faithful to being kind, tenderhearted, blameless, forgiving, and loving in our encounters with ourselves and others.

Remember to rule over sin, instead of sin enslaving you. If people willingly do certain sins, over time they subconsciously weaken themselves into submission of their enslavement to Satan. If Satan could freely take complete control of everyone, we all would be in a worse condition than the cities of Sodom and Gomorrah. Sodom and Gomorrah were ancient cities of Syria, located in the plain of Jordan. The cities were extremely perverted, corrupt, and evil. They were destroyed by fire, sent from Heaven, in the time of Abraham and Lot.

"Then, the Lord rained brimstone and fire on Sodom and Gomorrah,

from the Lord out of the heavens."

GENESIS 19:24

It is possible to build a loving life, where you experience more fruits-of-the-Spirit interactions, instead of a life ruled by sin and Satan's harassment. Start with developing a loving relationship with the Kingdom of God, which includes the Father, the Son, the Holy Spirit, and Holy Angels. To feel balanced in loving others, we should also apply self-love to ourselves. Nourish your body, soul, and spirit daily with love. You will become fueled with much love and energy to abundantly express love to all others. If we do not nourish ourselves, and instead we are neglectful, we may become prone to sickness and oppression, and the soul may become too impaired to adequately express love to others.

GOD CREATED HUMANS OUT OF HIS PERFECT LOVE

"Then God said, 'Let Us make man in Our image, according to

Our likeness; let them have dominion over the fish of the sea, over the birds

of the air, and over the cattle, over all the earth and over every creeping thing

that creeps on the earth.' So God created man in His own image; in the image

of God He created him; male and female He created them."

GENESIS 1:26-27

Having an awareness of all three parts of the self is a great start to nourishing yourself with love. In the beginning, God created souls, commonly known as humans. A soul consists of a spiritual heart and mind, which includes thoughts, words, emotions, images, and free will. A soul lives inside a physical body on earth. The soul's choices can impact the physical body's health and its life span. The soul itself is invisible to most human eyes, just like air and energy. Souls also have a spirit. The reborn spirit is steadily available to receive communication from God and God's Kingdom. The spirit can help the soul walk in the likeness of God.

When a soul is born, the soul is given two births from Almighty God. One is a physical birth in a physical body and the other is the choice for the spirit to be reborn, which is the gateway for the soul to receive eternal life with God. The soul's spirit is also invisible to most human eyes. A soul comes to earth with a choice to have a reborn spirit by accepting Jesus Christ as his or her Lord and Savior (John 3:16; Romans 10:9-10). I will discuss in other chapters the extraordinariness of forming a relationship with Jesus Christ.

The soul, along with its spirit, travels a narrow road toward God's eternal living. Our God is a loving and just God. If the soul has been given the opportunities and the mental ability to choose for his or her spirit to be reborn (for example, a two-year-old baby does not have the mental ability to choose to be reborn, but a functional-minded adult does), but rejects the invitations for redemption, then when Judgement Day comes, the soul will be forever separated from God and all of God's gifts. God's gifts include love, joy, peace, patience, kindness, goodness, faithfulness, gentleness, self-control; freedom from pain, fear, sadness, and disappointment; protection, fun, enjoyable activities, honesty, lots of laughter, purity, and mansions. All that is good and righteous comes from and stays with God. Grievously, God will be separated from the soul and the soul will be left in what is described as a torturous eternity.

Why must humans' spirits be reborn? Is it not an automatic rebirth when he or she arrives on earth?

In the beginning, when everything was good and perfect for man, Adam and Eve were freely given many gifts, including the opportunity for everlasting life. However, because Adam and Eve fell into sin, many of their blessings ended.

"Behold, the man has become like one of Us, to know good and evil. And now, lest he put out his hand and take also of the tree of life, and eat, and live forever."

GENESIS 3:22

Let us talk about what took place spiritually for humans because Eve sinned. She could no longer think solely with a pure and righteous heart and mind. Now, within her was an appetite for sin. Instead of Eve approaching Adam with guilt and remorse for being unfaithful and disobedient to God, she desired to do more sin, by tempting Adam to sin. Eve and Adam also stole, because they ate something that did not belong to them and were told upfront that they should not eat it. Sin was now a part of them and has passed on spiritually to each generation thereafter: "For there is not a just man on earth who does good and does not sin," (Ecclesiastes 7:20).

As an example, humans have way more than 10,000 thoughts a day. Some are sinful, which we entertain in our hearts and minds.

God knew sin was now within Adam and Eve. It was mandatory for God to act immediately and make certain changes for everyone's protection. Knowledge and the possible appetite for evil was within them now, and under no circumstances could evil live forever and serve alongside God and His Kingdom. God had no choice but to strip some of man's power and gifts and establish more rules and boundaries. It was for the best.

God is so loving. Although Adam's and Eve's spirits died early, God allowed Adam's and Eve's souls to live in their physical body for an exceptionally long time. God also allowed His Spirit to continue to be accessible to humans while there on earth to encourage them to rule over sin.

"And the Lord God commanded the man, saying, 'Of every tree of the garden you may freely eat; but of the tree of the knowledge of good and evil you shall not eat, for in the day that you eat of it you shall surely die.'"

GENESIS 2:16-17

"And the LORD said, 'My Spirit shall not strive with man forever, for he is indeed flesh; yet his days shall be one hundred and twenty years.'"

GENESIS 6:3

Adam and Eve lost a lot of blessings. Those gifts were replaced with challenges, demons, and curses they brought upon themselves and future generations.

"Then to Adam He said, 'Because you have heeded to the voice of your wife, and have eaten from the tree of which I commanded you, saying, "You shall not eat of it"; cursed is the ground for your sake; in toil you shall eat of it all the days of your life.'"

GENESIS 3:17

Just as we inherit physical traits from our parents, we also inherit spiritual traits. Adam and Eve passed on a spiritual "birth defect," which was the inheritance of a sinful appetite, demons, and a spirit that needs to be reborn. God knew the sins that were passed on, and our loving and merciful God made a great effort to encourage righteousness, but humans continued to sin terribly from generation to generation.

> *"Then the Lord saw that the wickedness of man was great in the earth, and that every intent of the thoughts of his heart was only evil continually."*
>
> GENESIS 6:5

OUR SIN REQUIRES THE ULTIMATE ACT OF LOVE: JESUS CHRIST

God's heart was troubled, and God decided to get rid of all the evil people, which was almost everyone. Noah and his family were saved. The book of Genesis describes Noah as an obedient servant of God among the people of his time. While the rest of the world was taken over by evil and violence, Noah was the only true follower of God left on earth. God decided to get rid of all the evil people, but Noah's life and his family's lives were spared. As time moved along, Noah grew old and died, and many other generations were born. Humans failed, again, to live by the laws and be righteous in their actions. Instead, they greatly repeated the prior generational sins. There were plenty of humans on earth and not a single person was without sin.

The wages for mankind's sin are death, but God, being so loving and merciful, created a solution. God allowed His only begotten Son, Jesus Christ, whom He loves dearly, who is perfect and sinless, to be a sacrificial offering and pay the debt for humans' sin. Jesus Christ came to earth to be our Lord and Savior. Jesus fulfilled the laws and taught humans how to love and how to rule over sin. Jesus Christ died on the cross to pay for everyone's sins and He was resurrected three days later. His resurrection gave those who believe Jesus is Lord and Savior the ability to repent and be forgiven of sins, the debt of death removed, the ability for our spirits to be reborn, the cleansing from curses, and the deliverance from demons and illnesses.

Allow me to say this again. God made it possible for humans who believe that Jesus is their Lord and Savior to have these abilities:

- Repent and be forgiven of sins.

- Be cleansed from curses, demons, and illness.

- Rule over sin and no longer be ruled by sin.

- Walk in the fruits of the Spirit.

- Receive an inheritance of a righteous bloodline.

A spirit that is reborn lives forever in Heaven with God, surrounded by love, joy, kindness, goodness, faithfulness, and peace. Other things that await us in Heaven are mansions and diamonds, as well as no more crying, pain, or sadness.

> *"And so it is written, 'The first man Adam became a living being.'*
> *The last Adam became a life-giving spirit."*
> 1 CORINTHIANS 15:45

Adam passed on the inheritance of our souls being born on earth, and Jesus passed on the opportunity for us to be reborn spirits who have eternal life with Almighty God.

There you have it! If you have accepted Jesus Christ as your Lord and Savior, rejoice.

> *"For the law of the Spirit of life in Christ Jesus has made*
> *me free from the law of sin and death."*
> ROMANS 8:2

THE REBORN SPIRIT CHECKLIST

- Honestly confess to Jesus you are a sinner. Truly confess and repent all sins you are aware and unaware that you have done.

- Sincerely ask Jesus to come into your life. Truly confess with belief John 3:16, which says, "For God so loved the world that He gave His only begotten Son, that whoever believes in Him should not perish but have everlasting life."

- Ask for forgiveness and forgive others.

- Get baptized with the Holy Spirit. Take courses on self-deliverance from demons or obtain deliverance from demons by someone ordained by God.

- Turn away from sin. Walk daily in the fruits of the Spirit (Galatians 5:22-23) and rule over sin as Jesus Christ, our Savior, taught us.

Chapter Four

SHARE THE TRUTH AND WIN SOULS TO JESUS CHRIST

"And He said to them, 'Go into all the world

and preach the gospel to every creature.'"

MARK 16:15

I f you believe without a doubt that Jesus is our Lord and Savior, you are a wise soul.

If there is any doubt that Jesus is our Lord and Savior, sincerely pray for God to provide you the truth in the best way possible so that you may receive the truth.

As believers, one of our greatest jobs on earth is to share the truth with unbelievers. Jesus Christ is the way, the truth, and the light. As you share with unbelievers, be according to the fruits of the Spirit, which is to be of love, joy, peace, patience, kindness, goodness, faithfulness, gentleness, and self-control. If possible, strive every day to walk in the fruits of the Spirit. Take the lead and start a conversation with questions that encourage a non-believer to share their life's needs and goals. Once you discover this, share what accepting Jesus Christ into their life can do for their life's goals.

KINDLY AND GENTLY INITIATE A CONVERSATION

Share what God has done for you since you accepted His Son, Jesus Christ, as your Lord and Savior. Testify about your blessings. Some examples might include sharing stories of healing, good health, peace beyond understanding, protection, miracles, wealth, mercy, overcoming addictions, escaping death, and other blessings God has bestowed upon you or someone you know. Share what spending quality time praising God has done for your heart and mind.

ASK SHARING QUESTIONS INSTEAD OF SHUT-DOWN QUESTIONS TO DISCOVER A NON-CHRISTIAN'S GOALS, WANTS, AND NEEDS

Invite the unbeliever to share what practices they use in life in order to live prosperously. *What do they use to feel safe? What do they do to experience peace and love? What ways do they choose to experience joy and happiness? When they leave earth, where do they expect to go? Who or what do they exercise their faith toward and how?*

These are *sharing* questions, which encourage details and explanations. This allows you to discover their needs, whereas *shut-down* questions allow for a "yes" or "no" response, which gives an opportunity for the unbeliever to shut down further questions before you discover their needs. Discovering the unbeliever's needs allows you to share with them specifically what God can provide within their life. Below are some more examples.

EXAMPLES OF SHARING QUESTIONS

- *What do you believe you would lose if you became a born-again Christian?*

- *What does Christianity mean to you?*

- *What are your views on having faith?*

- *What are your views on Jesus Christ dying on the cross and paying the wages for mankind's sin?*

- *Where do you believe you will go after you die?*

EXAMPLES OF SHUT-DOWN QUESTIONS

- *Do you believe you would lose out on things if you became a born-again Christian?*

- *Are you a Christian?*

- *Do you believe in faith?*

- *Do you believe Jesus Christ died on the cross for mankind's sins?*

- *Do you believe in life after death?*

DISCOVER WHAT BLOCKS THE TRUTH FROM AN UNBELIEVER

As you ask sharing questions, seek to discover the blockage that is preventing the truth from being unveiled to the unbeliever.

SHARE THE BLESSING OF ACCEPTING JESUS CHRIST

Throughout this book, you will read true stories about Christians receiving deliverance from strongholds and sexual immorality, healing from cancer, receiving forgiveness, exceptional peace, pure love, and joy, deliverance from demons, answers to financial struggles, healing from broken hearts, salvation from suicide, and more. Share the inspirational stories in this book with unbelievers who may have similar needs.

SHARE THE URGENCY

Tomorrow is not promised to any of us. Feel confident about where you are going after life on earth. It can be forever in God's Kingdom, surrounded by love and prosperity. At most, life on earth is around one hundred years or so, and then life on earth is over and life, with or without God, will be forever and ever and ever. Choose God.

PRESENT THE OFFER

Present the offer of how accepting Jesus Christ into their heart as their Lord and Savior, repenting and turning their attention away from sin, and walking in the fruits of the Spirit can orchestrate great changes in their life on earth and seal an eternal life of love, happiness, and prosperity with God and His Kingdom for eternal life.

Part Two

UNDERSTANDING GOD'S EXTRAORDINARY ENERGY

Chapter Five

ENERGY: AN EXTRAORDINARY GIFT FROM GOD

"That energy is God's energy, an energy deep within you, God himself willing and working at what will give him the most pleasure."

PHILIPPIANS 2:13 MSG

O ne day, an elderly client was explaining to me how serious she is about saving money. She went on to say that some people do not realize that although they turned the power off on an iron, a laptop, et cetera, if the device remains plugged in the electrical outlet, energy is still flowing and raising a person's electric bill. Her words echoed in my thoughts, reminding me about a person being unaware of how much their well-being and relationships are impacted by energy from their behaviors.

First, let us discuss how energy is commonly known to society. Energy is an invisible, powerful force, which provides the ability for God's creations to move from place to place, do work, make changes, and exist in different forms. Just like air is invisible and not greatly mentioned in the Bible but is immensely powerful and required for us to live on earth, the same goes for energy.

The results of energy are very visible. God has generously provided energy in all of His creations, and man has become aware of how to utilize energy in extraordinary ways. The beautiful sun has powerful energy, which does extraordinary work on earth. For example, the sun provides its solar energy to our land, which changes to another type of energy that contributes to the seeds growing to become a plant, the plant growing to become an apple tree, a pecan tree, or another tree. Humans eat the fruits, vegetable, or nuts and obtain energy from God's food. The energy from God's food contributes to humans, who grow from a fetus to a child, and then to an adult, actively moving around and doing work. Without God's generosity of energy, God's creations could not move, do work, make changes, or change to a different form. Nothing could reproduce.

Humans have extraordinary types of energy. Let's talk about energy in the physical body and the spiritual body.

ENERGY IN THE PHYSICAL BODY

Some examples of people exerting a lot of physical energy include the top salesperson who talks fast, moves fast, and performs at the level of three employees, kids playing endlessly, and marathon runners. People who possess a low level of physical energy may feel tired easily, frequently struggle to get out of bed, and prefer to sit down all day. The good news is that God has provided us many ways to possess lots of energy, which manifests into motivation to get up, do God's work, and have lots of fun, and strengthens our free will so we may win spiritual battles. For example, we might exercise, move around throughout the day, pray to and worship God, memorize scriptures, weight train, do aerobics, dance to upbeat Christian music, or intermediate fast (check with a physician). The proper amount of sleep, healthy food, refraining from over-eating, staying hydrated, and maintaining a positive attitude can help fuel our physical bodies with energy.

GOD CREATED HUMAN ENERGY

"I can do all things through Christ who strengthens me."

PHILIPPIANS 4:13

Our generous God allows humans to arrive on earth with an extraordinary energy. I refer to it as *love energy* from God. Our bodies are equipped with powerful energy and being that we are of God's image, this means the energy for us is powerful *love energy*. The love energy which surrounds the exterior part of the body, I refer to as body covering. All of God's creations have energy. Love energy is the most powerful energy of all. If you doubt, consult the experts, such as doctors and scientists. God created the human body to be so powerful and full of life. It is God's powerful breath in our lungs.

"And the Lord God formed man of the dust of the ground, and breathed into his nostrils the breath of life; and man became a living being."

GENESIS 2:7

God has designed us with powerful, energized bodies to help protect us while we are on earth.

Many of us can attest from our own personal experiences or witnessing others who have abused their bodies for decades—with drugs, alcohol, fights, a lot of medical problems, unhealthy eating, obesity, and toxins from jealousy, unforgiveness, anger, and rage—they are still standing strong with powerful energy within them. We are of God's image. We are powerful. Our energy, internal organs, and immune systems are extraordinary. The human body can tolerate many years of non-loving behaviors to the body and mind before most people's powerful energy begins to dissipate. Many people use the excuse of simply getting old. If we live in the image of God, by walking in the fruits of the Spirit, we can maximize more powerful experiences. Our powerful bodies can help rule over demonic forces and health problems, which can help us to reduce the grieving of the Holy Spirit and Holy Angels. God has really made us of great power, and our job is to show appreciation by walking in love and thanking God daily for our many blessings.

However, for the sins we discussed before (sexually immorality, sensuality, idolatry, sorcery, enmity, strife, jealousy, fits of anger, rivalries, dissensions, divisions, envy, drunkenness, orgies, and other behaviors like these), repetitiously doing those type of sins can cause a person's energy to negatively change and receive tears and holes. This puts oneself at a higher risk for illness, accidents, et cetera, because the body covering, which is energy surrounding the exterior part of you that helps shield you from harm within your surroundings, has been impacted due to your behaviors, including unwilful behaviors, such as assaults, violations, over extended grieving, et cetera. As a result, holes and tears occur within the body covering, leaving the body open and vulnerable to more problems, but love, love, love, as much as possible, forgiveness, and assistance from the Holy Spirit, can help recover your energy and heal those holes and tears. Thank God, our Heavenly Father, who has mercy on our sinful nature, as we sin and sin again. God is so forgiving and merciful. God is so intelligent. He has already orchestrated the restoration of our energy and our powerful bodies. The Holy Spirit can heal and restore our energy within our powerful bodies. We can also heal through fasting, praying, repenting of our sins, renouncing of demons, righteously loving everyone, and exercising our will by using faith and asking in the name of Jesus with the power of the Holy Spirit to heal all parts of us.

GOD CREATED ENERGY WITHIN LOVING BEHAVIORS

Loving behaviors are one of humanity's extraordinary resources to maximize experiencing God's powerful love energy. Whether we are aware or unaware, we are constantly choosing a type of energy, which impacts our health and relationships. The effect from energy can take seconds, minutes, days, weeks, or years.

What energy are you releasing through your thoughts, words, emotions, images, and actions?

EXTRAORDINARY POWER!

If the energy is from interacting on the fruits-of-the-Spirit level, which is the heart and mind applying action to reciprocate love, joy, peace, patience, kindness, goodness, faithfulness, gentleness, and self-control, then the fruits of the Spirit will manifest results. The soul will clearly interpret information from the soul's spirit and the Holy Spirit more often. The team of armored Holy Angels will be readily available to communicate to you in the most extraordinary ways. Your prayers will rapidly move to the 3rd Heaven, you will have greater strength to resolve challenges, greater strength to renounce demons and rebuke sin, more stamina to build loving relationships and accomplish more goals, and the ability to naturally experience your feel-good chemicals more often, like endorphins, oxytocin, and serotonin. Energy from God's loving behaviors are underrated. Many people can experience loving behaviors and their energy. However, it is the reborn Christian who has been given power by the Holy Spirit to consistently walk in the fruits of the Spirit and who experiences the fastest and most powerful energy the most.

During the pending stage of my contract to purchase a new property, I learned about an appraisal contingency clause that I could have implemented, which allowed me to back out of the contract without financial penalty, if the appraisal estimate was less than the offer. I felt frustrated because that option was not presented to me. In the past, my frustration would have turned into incredible anger, followed by a pounding headache and a lack of energy. My words and behaviors would have not been what Paul encourages in Titus 3:2: "To speak evil of no one, to be peaceable, gentle, showing all humility to all men." However, to walk in the fruits of the Spirit often helps to develop within me the strength to exercise self-control and seek God for a peaceful resolution.

So, instead of calling my realtor and aggressively complaining, I used my energy to pray. I repented for my frustration that was driven by fear. I took accountability for my carelessness in not being more educated about my options and asked God for help to forgive my realtor and myself. I asked God for a peaceful resolution, the healing of my heart, and the removal of my fears.

The next day, the appraisal's results stated that the property value was about $1,000 more than what was being offered. I praised God for a prosperous and peaceful completion of the purchase.

Energy from loving thoughts, words, emotions, images, and actions move within our lives with far greater power than energy from non-loving behaviors. Love energies move you further from Satan's lower vibrations and his territories, so you may surpass obstacles, barriers, and problems.

These love energies are rapidly moving and circling around you and act as a reward from all the love released by applying loving thoughts, words, emotions, images, and actions. Energy from loving behaviors moves in the spiritual world with power and speed that is far greater than the power of the speed of light. Understandably so because God is the Creator of light and God is love. No other energy moves near as fast or as strong as the energy from love. God is love and love is from God, so it only makes sense for love energy to be the most powerful energy of all energies. We are of God's image. We are designed to be powerful reproducers on earth.

PROTECT YOUR ENERGY FROM NON-LOVING BEHAVIORS

It started out as an ordinary night. In the 1990s, David and his wife Joanne stopped by his friend's recording studio to work on a song that David was currently recording. Once they arrived, it was common for his wife to mingle with the other artists' wives or girlfriends. Most of the time, Joanne shared drinks and laughter with the owner's girlfriend Kathy.

As the hours passed and people went home, Joanne and Kathy went outside to sit inside Joanne's Bronco. Kathy lit up some marijuana and they started getting high. As usual, Joanne, who got high almost every day, took several hits and began to feel a sedative-like state of relaxation. But this sedative-like state was not for long, as this time it felt like she drifted far into another dimension. She could see into the spiritual world, as clear as she could hear and see Kathy. Joanne could hear and see very tall and ugly demons that were standing next to her. They were yelling evil words and cursing at Joanne.

She screamed, "Jesus, please help me!"

Kathy nervously grabbed Joanne, asking, "What is wrong?"

As she franticly tried to respond, Joanne watched the demons and what felt like another dimension vanish. Still frantic, she yelled for her husband to take her home, as she pleaded to God for deliverance.

That was the last time she ever did any drugs. Joanne realized she was blessed. She later realized just how blessed. Some medical experts say that certain drugs can sometimes affect the pineal gland in such a way. This effect is commonly known to some as the third eye opening, which allows a human to see into the spiritual world. This is horrifying to see and hear if you are indulging in sins, such as drugs, alcohol, immoral sex and sex fantasies, unrighteous anger, and other similar sins, because those behaviors are of lower energy vibrations. This means they are rooted in sin, of which Satan is currently territorial and holds legal access to sinners.

Joanne's childhood neighbor had the same experience from getting high, but unfortunately, he continued to do drugs. One day, while getting high, he passed out and when he had awakened in the hospital, the demons and their evil voices did not leave. He was taken to a psychiatric facility. The last she heard, he had stopped taking his medicine, continued to hear and see demons, and had run away from his caregivers and now lives homeless on the streets.

Certain non-loving behaviors, such as getting high like Joanne's childhood neighbor, allow the possibility for Satan to have dominion in the sinner's life. However, loving behaviors make it possible for God's power to help change the direction of our lives and rule over sin.

Unlike loving behaviors, non-loving behaviors are the opposite of the fruits of the Spirit. They weaken your energy to a lower vibration, of which Satan is territorial and has the rights of dominion over sin. For example, non-loving behaviors and sins like hate, anger, fear, jealousy, selfishness, extended grieving, drug abuse, alcohol abuse, food binging, illnesses, depression, lying, cheating, immoral sexual activity, and others have lower and problematic energy. Many people have experienced these behaviors briefly; however, we all should live a lifestyle that avoids seething in these types of behaviors. These behaviors can weaken your energy, causing one to have less protection from injury, illness, trauma, and accidents.

Non-loving behaviors by others can greatly weaken a person's energy. These behaviors include theft, gossip, verbal abuse, manipulation, cheating, bullying, and unwilful fornication. An example of unwilful fornication is molestation, rape, or other sexual acts without consent. When a person experiences feeling violated, his or her energy is impaired. Many times, just like other sins, demons are behind the scenes, instigating the violator to do such a sexually immoral act. The victim has rights to take legal action. God will deal with the violator. As the violation takes place, although unwilful by the victim, sexually immoral spirits transmit to the victim. Many women and men who are promiscuous, who sometimes work at escort services, the porn industry, and other similar places, have experienced unwilful fornication at an incredibly young age. Unbeknown to the victims, sexual demons stayed around, planting seeds to influence the victim to create a lifestyle of sexual immorality within themselves. They often have not experienced true deliverance, healing, or forgiveness from the assault. Thank God, all victims can be healed and delivered from sexual demons. Thank you, Holy Spirit, for being available to call on for healing and to help the victims experience forgiveness.

No human is perfect, but the Holy Spirit is perfect and available with perfect solutions and healing. Born-again Christians have so many God-given resources to live a beautiful life. Let us maximize our gifts from God.

COMMON SUBTLE BEHAVIORS THAT WEAKEN YOUR ENERGY

Someone who feels too oppressed to get up and out of bed could be experiencing strongholds from Satan, along with the strong sensation to stay in bed when it is in their best interest to get up and go to work, exercise, pray, or clean up. That individual is probably receiving negative thoughts and strong urges from the spirits of laziness, prompting them to stay in bed and avoid exercise, work, praying, and cleaning up. These are all activities that provide the body and soul with energy.

However, lounging for an extended time in bed and not doing physically productive activities does not help you generate energy. It helps Satan systematically plot to weaken your energy. If your energy is weak, the chances of you doing hours of intercessory prayer for many people who are being attacked or held in Satan's bondage is highly unlikely. The chances of you working to win souls to Christ are highly unlikely. Satan knows if you're idle or lazy, and especially over time, your energy is weakened. This often results in your day just consisting of self-gratifying behaviors, such as watching television, listening to music, looking at social media, gaming, or just lounging around, with your mind being flooded with unproductive thoughts and words. You can become more susceptible to being judgmental, greedy, a gossiper, sexually immoral, and succumbing to other similar sins. This strengthens Satan to rule within you, making it feel extremely hard to turn from sin. But we are so blessed to be able to sincerely repent, receive deliverance, and turn toward love.

Rebuke and replace demons with fasting (upon doctor's approval) and do the opposite of idle behaviors or laziness, such as getting up earlier, cleaning a room in the house, or simply cleaning a section of the room.

Start your day earlier. Spend more quality time with God. Do something that is the opposite of what demons are tempting you to do. Take baby steps to allow adequate time for the subconscious mind to replace the old habit with a new habit. Soon, you will have new productive habits. Demons will flee. When they return, rebuke again and implement healthy habits to replace the old sinful habit.

Recognize the sin in what is happening and say, in the name of Jesus with the power of the Holy Spirit, "I renounce you, spirit of laziness." Replace Satan's temptation with a relatable scripture that you can memorize. For example, as you resist the temptation to lay in bed, say Philippians 4:13, "I can do all things through Christ who strengthens me."

Satan and his team of demons are always moving throughout the earth for an opportunity to set a trap for people to become oppressed. As you consistently resist sin, they must flee. Sins such as idleness, gluttony, little white lies, and sexual fantasies may all seem not too harmful. However, sins can invite problems, demons, and a change of energy. The energy of sinful, non-loving behaviors is much lower energy than loving behaviors, which makes a person more susceptible to demons of lower vibrations. The weaker your energy is, the greater the opportunity for demons to influence you or bog you down with temptations, problems, and frustrations. Then, it becomes easier to sin, and the sin grows larger and larger, as Satan continues to hang around, laying a ploy for sin to overtake and rule you.

The good news is God is always ready and waiting for you, so do not give up. Even if you are currently ruled by sin, you can pray, love, repent, love, pray, love, believe, love, and pursue the Holy Spirit with all your strength and love. You will break free. Love can cover a multitude of sins.

Chapter Six

FIVE WAYS GOD COMMUNICATES HIS EXTRAORDINARY ENERGY

Here are more powerful gifts from God to enrich us with energy so that we may live productive and righteous lives. They are *thoughts, words, emotions, images,* and *actions.* We use them to communicate with the Father, the Son, the Holy Spirit, Holy Angels, other people, and ourselves.

Each communicator has energy, and energy provides humans and animals with the ability to move, vibrate high or low, make changes to our lives, change to different forms, and do work. Coming up in this book are examples of ways the fruits-of-the-Spirit behaviors can be applied through our thoughts, words, emotions, images, and actions, which are gateways to navigate God's love energy.

Energy from loving behaviors is the fastest energy to move our thoughts, words, emotions, images, and actions to their intended location.

This energy is more likely to help resolve relationship issues and achieve goals. Energy from non-loving behaviors is problematic, which can interfere with achieving your goals.

So, I ask you, *what are you communicating? What are you expecting in return?*

God provides us with the ability to communicate love to the world.

ENERGY IN THOUGHTS

"Finally, brethren, whatever things are true, whatever things are noble, whatever things are just, whatever things are pure, whatever things are lovely, whatever things are of good report, if there is any virtue and if there is anything praiseworthy—meditate on these things."

PHILIPPIANS 4:8

Energy moves your thoughts to their point of destination. Loving thoughts can travel an infinite distance, moving rapidly to Heaven. Our thoughts can contribute to a goal, which can change into a physical form through the usage of energy in applying faith and work. Everything God created started with a thought. The sun, trees, animals, humans, and everything else all began with a thought. Humans are of God's image, and therefore we can co-create on earth using our thoughts as one of our resources. The complete process of thoughts changing to physical form is not visible. However, speaking words of faith, maintaining emotions of belief, creating detailed images of your thoughts, and physically working daily to manifest opportunities for your thoughts to change into physical form are all empowered by you. Take charge of your thoughts when you initially awake. Immediately choose to walk in the Spirit, such as giving praise to the Father, the Son, the Holy Spirit, and Holy Angels. Say thank you daily for what they do for us. Read the Bible and pray to keep your mind on God. Recite within your mind all the generous things Jesus did while on earth. Pray for yourself and others. Memorize scripture that inspires you to maintain positive thoughts. Practice maintaining positive thoughts for your circumstances.

For example, if you are dissatisfied with your current home and desire to buy a new home, imagine that your current residence is exactly how you desire your new house. Apply daily thoughts toward your new home. Stay faithful by paying the rent and maintaining the upkeep of your current residence. Appreciate your current bedroom, bathroom, kitchen stove, and other things you use daily. Maintain being loving, joyful, peaceful, patient, kind, good, faithful, gentle, and self-controlled in your current obligations. Start a plan of action to reach your goal of buying a new home. The energy from these behaviors will increase the flow of opportunities for the things you are working toward to manifest. If we neglect our current obligations, by not paying our bills or disrespecting the landlord's property, and are unappreciative of our current possessions, the energy from those non-loving behaviors can create problematic consequences, which may distract us and interfere with reaching our goals. Those problematic distractions can interrupt you from being available when opportunities arrive for you to accomplish your goals.

As soon as you wake, create positive thoughts. Move past any negative thoughts. Energy provides the ability for thoughts to move from place to place. Your thoughts can travel to Heaven, to the Holy Spirit and Holy Angels, your family, friends, coworkers, and others. Throughout the day, evaluate the type of thoughts you are vibrating outward. Are your thoughts loving? Set an alarm to evaluate your current thoughts throughout the day.

For example, set your phone alarm to go off at different times and review if your thoughts have the energy vibration of the fruits of the Spirit.

Positive Thoughts in Your Household

One morning, I woke up to the song, "Beautiful Day," by Jamie Grace playing in my head. As I got dressed and went about my day, I spoke with my daughter around brunch-time, and she was singing the same song. The song came into her thoughts first thing in the morning. I chuckled and told her I woke up with the same song playing in my head. My daughter woke up a few hours before me that morning. I believe "Beautiful Day" was surfacing within the air of our home that morning. The song is a Christian song that I appreciate hearing in my thoughts. If it had been a song influencing me to sin, I could have simply changed my thoughts in seconds to a Christian song. Energy allows us to change our thoughts, words, emotions, images, and actions instantaneously.

Similarly, one day, Taylor and her mom were driving to the grocery store. Taylor shared with her mom that she started reading the entire Bible again and was currently reading Genesis 12. Her mom was speechless because she told Taylor that she was also currently reading Genesis. She had started a week prior. They both were amazed that they were inspired with the same idea at the same time. Who initiated the thought within the house? Was it Taylor, her mom, the Holy Angels, the Holy Spirit, or the thoughts of others sent to them? This is an example of entertaining loving thoughts within a household.

Negative Thoughts in Your Household

Jay was twenty years old, and his younger brother Brandon was a teenager at the time. While Jay lay on their sofa, he noticed the wire of a cell phone charger that was exposed and hanging. He had a thought to grab the wire and put it in his mouth. He did not question his thoughts. He was not drunk, high, or feeling unstable. Instead of questioning why he would even have such a thought, he went ahead and touched the end of the wire with the tip of his tongue.

"Ouch!" Jay said loudly.

Jay's brother Brandon turned around and looked at him, noticing that he threw the wire on the floor. Brandon first asked if he was okay. Jay said yes. Brandon went on to chuckle and ask, "Did you just put the wire in your mouth?" Jay said yes. Brandon chuckled again and said, "Earlier today, I sat in that chair and did the same thing."

This story is an example of thoughts residing within a household. They may come from familiar demons lurking around the home. They may come from people. The average person may sometimes feel as if the thought is his very own; however, thoughts can also be sent to you or already be surfacing within your environment. Should we respond to every thought that surfaces within our minds? No. Praise God! Every thought has a certain level of energy attached to it when we receive it. If they are loving thoughts, the energy is most powerful.

What Type of Energy Is in Your Household?

What type of energy from families' and friends' thoughts are surfacing within our households? Is it powerful love and productive energy, or exceptionally low and problematic energy? Experts say that humans have thousands of thoughts a day. There are habitual thoughts that our subconscious minds repeatedly send to us.

Memorize loving scriptures and loving affirmations to add to your daily thoughts. Therefore, as you repetitiously say loving scriptures daily, your subconscious mind will record them and effortlessly resurface them to your memory as a daily habit. Stay conscious that your thoughts have energy, and if it is a righteous, loving thought that includes faith, then God's energy will be utilized in moving good things toward you. If thoughts are the opposite of God's loving thoughts, then things that are opposite of love will be associated with your thoughts and will move in your direction. God, Jesus, the Holy Spirit, Holy Angels, and unfortunately, demons can send us thoughts. Other people's thoughts can be sent to you, which explains how many children growing up in a household often are on the same energy level with the same shared views and thought processes as others in the household.

Create a location in your home where you choose only productive thoughts. For example, you might choose a room to pray to God in the name of Jesus, or where kids can do their homework. Not to say that other thoughts are not able to travel there, but if the location is only used for being productive, such as doing homework, praying, and memorizing scriptures, then the energy will strengthen for productive thoughts to dominate in that location. It is more challenging for a child to focus on studying in the living room in front of a television or a game room where all types of thoughts resonate. As you apply walking-in-the-Spirit behaviors to your thoughts, words, emotions, images and actions, your soul will be able to decipher thoughts sent from God, Satan, others, and the self.

How does that positively impact our children? When a child starts spending less time with his family and starts spending more time with others, the environment a child spends a lot of time in may become an influence on a child's views and thought processes, whether good or bad. Train your child to send and receive loving thoughts. Discern and reject negative thoughts as a precaution toward Satan's potential attacks. It is a good idea to regularly discuss thoughts, words, emotions, images, and actions with your children.

Imagine your thoughts moving around your household, to and from your family members. Have you ever pondered about eating an Italian dish for dinner, and thirty minutes later, your spouse came in the room, suggesting eating lasagna for dinner? What about hearing thoughts of a certain song, and soon after, you hear a family member singing the same song, because they were also having thoughts about the same song? It is beneficial to our families and friends when we all choose thoughts of the fruits of the Spirit. What thoughts do you encounter from your family members? Gently and objectively discuss your thoughts with family members. Pray for guidance before you begin. Pray to discern which thoughts are coming from the Kingdom of God, Satan, people, pets, and the self. I often tell people if your thoughts keep you walking in the fruits of the Spirit, those thoughts are probably from the Kingdom of God, intercessory prayers, loved ones, or the self. If they influence you to gratify the flesh, those thoughts are probably from the self, other people, or Satan's team. Strive to embrace thoughts that encourage you to walk in the fruits of the Spirit.

Memorize These Scriptures to Inspire Positive Thoughts

"And do not be conformed to this world, but be transformed by the renewing of your mind, that you may prove what is that good and acceptable and perfect will of God."

ROMANS 12:2

"You will keep him in perfect peace, whose mind is stayed on You, because he trusts in You." (Isaiah 26:3)

"Finally, brethren, whatever things are true, whatever things are noble, whatever things are just, whatever things are pure, whatever things are lovely, whatever things are of good report, if there is any virtue, and if there is anything praiseworthy—meditate on these things." (Philippians 4:8)

"How precious also are Your thoughts to me, O God! How great is the sum of them!" (Psalms 139:17)

"And be renewed in the spirit of your mind." (Ephesians 4:23)

"For to be carnally minded is death, but to be spiritually minded is life and peace." (Romans 8:6)

Examples of Positive Thoughts

- I hope everyone develops a close relationship with God, Jesus Christ, the Holy Spirit, and Holy Angels.

- Thank you, God, for the beautiful trees, which provide oxygen and absorb carbon dioxide for us.

- Today, I will spend joyful time with the Holy Spirit.

- We will experience a lot of laughter today.

- We will experience exceedingly kind people today.

- I will keep my thoughts on the present as much as possible.

List Your Five Most Frequent Positive Thoughts Below

1. _____

_____

2. _____

_____

3. _____

_____

4. _____

_____

5. _____

_____

ENERGY IN WORDS

"Let no corrupt word proceed out of your mouth, but what is good for necessary edification, that it may impart grace to the hearers."
EPHESIANS 4:29

Words can uplift, heal, and inspire, or they can offend or damage people and their relationships. Using edifying words with loving intentions can release powerful energy to the recipient, which encourages the recipient to feel inspired and motivated, which is nourishing to the soul. As reborn Christians, we have the authority in Jesus' name with the power of the Holy Spirit to heal the body, the mind, to win souls, and to cast demons out of our bodies using our faith and words.

When you wake each morning, claim your power to do great work through your words. Include in your morning prayer the following: "In Jesus' name, may all my words be for the good of the Kingdom of God. May my words bring healing to the soul and health to the body. May my words win souls to Christ, putting away anger, wrath, and slander, and expressing love."

Loving words, with belief in Christ, include love energy, which inspires happy emotions within us.

Have you ever noticed after reading of Jesus' promises with faith, you feel energized? The words in the Bible are full of life. Energy from a loving soul, who speaks life-giving words with faith, moves loving energy to its recipient effortlessly. This improves the recipient's state of being. There are many scriptures that instruct us to speak words according to the fruits of the Spirit, even during a conflict, to inspire a peaceful resolution. Learn and memorize scriptures that inspire you to say peaceful words during a time you may feel stressed.

A new Christian and choir member, Lisa, read the book of Titus, mainly in chapter 3, which says, "To speak evil of no one, to be peaceable, gentle, showing all humility to all men," (Titus 3:2-4). Reading this helped her to restrain the words she initially wanted to say to one of her choir members, Latrele, who was responsible for notifying the choir members of schedule changes. Latrele mistakenly did not inform Lisa that the current date and time had changed for choir rehearsal. This caused Lisa to unnecessarily get a babysitter and waste unnecessary money and time driving to rehearsal practice.

When Lisa arrived at practice and no one was there, she texted Latrele to inquire, "Where's everyone?"

Latrele said, "You obviously forgot. I sent a group text that the rehearsal date had been changed!"

Lisa had not received the group text. In error, Latrele inadvertently added the wrong phone number for Lisa in the choir group text. Not to mention, the correct process to invite and cancel choir rehearsal was an email invitation to attend rehearsal. An email notification was supposed to be sent whenever rehearsal was canceled or rescheduled. Lisa received the email to attend, but not an email that rehearsal was rescheduled.

Lisa's frustration could have easily subsided, if Latrele's words were not so full of blame, nonchalant, and unapologetic. Had Latrele's words been full of empathy and an apology, it could have helped Lisa's frustration subside quickly. Instead, it only fueled and extended Lisa's frustration. Because Latrele did not apologize, Lisa wanted to call and tell her that she was rude, insensitive, and a few other names, and how much inconvenience she had caused. But because Lisa felt too angry, her words would have probably been too damaging, and far from gentle, as Jesus instructs us to respond.

So, Lisa prayed, forgave Latrele, and read the doctrine of how Jesus wants us to respond when we are offended by our brothers and sisters. It was about two weeks before she communicated with Latrele and saw her again. Lisa's frustration had gone. Her and Latrele resumed exchanging kind words during rehearsals and performances. Had Lisa not turned to Jesus' instructions and instead attacked Latrele with harsh words, this conflict could have snowballed and created unnecessary tension between the two, such as health issues from all the toxic and harsh words, as well as prolonged frustration and unforgiveness within the body.

Let go and let God.

Avoid saying destructive words, which could harm your relationships with others. When you speak words of love, one can feel uplifted. Harsh words can cause a person to feel hurt, wounded, unloved, and if prolonged, can bring upon health issues like headaches, anxiety, and others. The energy of the person who said the unloving words circles around and has the ability to backlash. If you release loving words with faith, the energy from your loving words moves loving encounters toward you. When someone compliments you and gives you recognition, that energy from those loving behaviors goes within your body, touching your cells and tissues, and gives life to you.

What Happens to Us When We Hear Righteous, Loving Words?

Have you received words from a parent, coach, supervisor, motivational speaker, pastor, relative, or friend who uplifted you and suddenly you felt energized to achieve your goals? Have you encountered someone who said very hurtful words that crushed your spirit? Did you later experience feeling a headache, angry, stressed, or tired, and a few days later, the body went down with illness, such as a cold, allergies, a hoarse throat, a headache, or an outbreak on your skin? Think about this. If the body can become impaired from encountering hurtful words during an argument, what is happening to the body when we hear honest, uplifting, and righteous, loving words?

I believe words are powerful medicine for the body. Maintain good mental and physical health by maintaining words from the fruits of the Spirit in all your encounters. Experts say that humans speak an average of more than 10,000 words a day. Say positive words, affirmations, and scriptures each day. When we speak such words from the heart, we are turning on our feel-good chemicals, which cause us to feel uplifted, motivated, and appreciated. When we communicate harsh words, name-calling, or other unloving words, the low energy from those words moves problems to the body, the mind, and relationships.

Memorize Scriptures That Instruct You to Speak Loving Words and Say Them Daily

"There is one who speaks like the piercings of a sword,
but the tongue of the wise promotes health." (Proverbs 12:18)

"It is the Spirit who gives life; the flesh profits nothing. The words
that I speak to you are spirit, and *they* are life." (John 6:63)

"The heart of the wise teaches his mouth, and adds learning to his lips."
(Proverbs 16:23)

"Pleasant words are like a honeycomb, sweetness to the soul
and health to the bones." (Proverbs 16:24)

"He who guards his mouth preserves his life, but he who opens
wide his lips shall have destruction." (Proverbs 13:3)

"For by your words you will be justified, and by your words you
will be condemned." (Matthew 12:37)

Start Your Day Saying These Positive Words and Phrases

Abundant, Achieve, Acceptance, Accomplish, Accurate, Advance, Agreement, Allow, All Things, Always, Appreciate, Approved, Arrive Safely, Available, Awake, Awesome, Beautiful, Believe, Billions, Body, Brilliant, Brittany, Calm, Changes, Cheerful, Cheerfully Give, Comfort, Communicate, Count, Courageous, Current, Dashing, Delightful, Endurance, Energy, Engage, Everlasting, Everything, Exceed, Extraordinary, Faith, Family, Fellowship, First, Forever, Forgive, Fortune, Full, Free, Generous, Gentleness, God, Good Morning, Gorgeous, Grace, Grand, Great, Happy, Happiness, Healed, Healthy, Heaven, Holy, Holy Spirit, Honest, Honor, Hope, Humor, Feeling, Intentionality, Invite, Jesus, Joy, Justice, Kind, Learn, Life, Live, Love, Living, Marketable, Marriage, Modest, Money, More, Most, Multiple, Nice, Open, Opportunity, Optimistic, Overflowing, Paid in Full, Patience, Peace, People, Perfect Attendance, Perfect Credit, Positive, Potential, Prosperous, Prizes, Pure, Queen, Radiant, Relationship, Resolve, Rest, Rich, Safe, Sales, Self-Control, Self-Love, Sleep, Sweet, Successful, Talk, Teaching, Thank You, Understand, Unite, United, Universe, Victorious, Win, Work, Well, and Yes. Good morning, may I assist you? How are you doing today? My pleasure. I appreciate your time. Thank you for inquiring. Great job! Keep going, you're doing a great job. I believe in you. Anything is possible with God. Thank you for being who you are. I trust you with all my heart. You're awesome. I hope all is well. It's been a pleasure talking to you. I hope to see you soon. Excuse me, may I go through here? May I go ahead of you? Thank you so much. You are such an inspiration. I can always count on you. I understand, understandably so. Goodnight, sweetheart. Goodnight and I love you. Sweet dreams.

Now, It's Your Turn

Write as many positive words on this page as you can recollect.

_____

_____

_____

_____

_____

_____

_____

_____

_____

_____

_____

_____

_____

_____

ENERGY IN EMOTIONS

"But the fruit of the Spirit is love, joy, peace, longsuffering [patience], kindness,

goodness, faithfulness, gentleness, and self-control. Against such there is no law."

GALATIANS 5:22-23

God's goodness is shown through His generosity of emotions and its energy, which gives us the ability to continuously change our mood. Remember that energy allows us the ability to make changes. Could you imagine feeling frustrated and never being able to move past that feeling and onto happiness?

"I know that there is nothing better for people than to be happy

and to do good while they live."

ECCLESIASTES 3:12 NIV

How often are you happy? Good behaviors beget good emotions.

"And be kind to one another, tenderhearted, forgiving one another,

even as God in Christ forgave you."

EPHESIANS 4:32

Such behaviors above help to motivate us to stay connected to God as much as possible and resonate in continuous love energy. These behaviors allow the energy from love to move more happy encounters our way.

Here is an example of demonstrating kind emotions: If a motorist suddenly cut in front of you, to the point where you are basically tailgating the motorist, take a deep breath, extend peace by slowing down, forgive them, and let it go. Choose to stay at a kind and happy level. Sing praise and worship songs while you drive happily to your destination. The energy you release from that encounter is of patience, forgiveness, and kindness, and it will circle around and extend the same mercy to you when you unintentionally impact someone negatively. What do you choose to think, say, or do when a motorist cuts you off, or does other careless acts, and you feel a rush of anger? Do you retaliate with words? Do you harbor the anger?

Attempt with all your strength to allow these and similar emotions to pass through you. Such emotions are filled with toxic energy, which can circle around more encounters that will stimulate those toxic emotions within you and form a toxic lifestyle. Remember, where love is absent, Satan is probably present. Prolonged seething within those types of emotions can also release harmful toxins within you, which may cause you to be more likely to experience illness. It is unimaginable to completely avoid feeling angry, resentful, jealous, and the like; however, work hard to build a life as God instructs us and you will experience fewer toxic emotions and more bliss in your life. How often do you feel happy? How often do you experience feeling peaceful and complete? To experience a joyful lifestyle requires you to let go of toxic behaviors and move toward fruits-of-the-Spirit behaviors. Fruits-of-the-Spirit behaviors have an energy that is powerful, circling around encounters with people and animals. This energy offers you the opportunity to have loving encounters.

Emotions give us an awareness of the type of energy we have flowing within us. It is a blessing to be able to learn how to experience and maintain loving emotions. It is important to set the tone of how you feel when you awake from your sleep. Turn on your feel-good chemicals when you initially wake up. Whenever you encounter people, nature, or animals, choose within your heart and mind to walk in the fruits-of-the-Spirit thoughts, words, emotions, images, and actions. This will allow energy from those behaviors to flood you with love wherever you go.

The emotions I felt one Sunday morning were anything but joyful. I felt unhappy and not interested in going to church, but I went anyway. After I arrived and listened to the pastor's sermon, my emotions changed from apathetic to engaged and onto happiness. Afterwards, I said, "I am glad I went to church today." Energy allows our emotions to change from one emotion to another within seconds and to move from place to place. During church, I experienced the power of the Holy Spirit in the atmosphere. I experienced being uplifted by the pastor's words. I experienced the congregation's energy from their emotions moving throughout the atmosphere. What started out as sad emotions changed to joyful. Attend a loving, Bible-based church where the Holy Spirit is present.

Memorize and Say Scriptures Daily to Inspire God's Loving Behaviors Within Your Emotions

"A merry heart does good, *like* medicine,
but a broken spirit dries the bones." (Proverbs 17:22)

"For God has not given us a spirit of fear,
but of power and of love and of a sound mind." (2 Timothy 1:7)

"I will give you a new heart and put a new spirit within you; I will take the heart of stone out of your flesh and give you a heart of flesh."
(Ezekiel 36:26)

"This *is* the covenant that I will make with them after those days, says the Lord: I will put My laws into their hearts, and in their minds I will write them." (Hebrews 10:16)

"A wrathful man stirs up strife,
but *he who is* slow to anger allays contention." (Proverbs 15:18)

"A fool vents all his feelings, but a wise
man holds them back." (Proverbs 29:11)

"I know there is nothing better for people than to be happy and to do
good while they live." (Ecclesiastes 3:12 NIV)

"He heals the brokenhearted and binds up their wounds." (Psalm 147:3)

ENERGY IN IMAGES

"Where there is no vision, the people perish: but he that keepeth the law, happy is he."
PROVERBS 29:18 KJV

God Gifts Us with Images to Help Us

We can receive visions as warnings, instructions, and edification. The low
energy world consists of witches, psychics, Satanists, manipulators, and
other misguided individuals, who often receive deceitful visions from
Satan and his demonic kingdom. These deceitful visions often lead these
individuals and others whom they influence further from learning that
Jesus is our Lord and Savior. However, believers who apply faith and walk
in the fruits of the Spirit can manifest the most rapid and powerful results
from God's visions.

God Gifts Us with Images to Edify Us

When I was a little girl, my maternal grandmother died. My family
attended her funeral, while I stayed with a babysitter. They felt I was too
young to attend the funeral. I was sad that I could not attend. As I was
laying on my bed, crying, I looked up and saw a vision of my grandmother's

face, appearing in the air and close to the ceiling. She had a gleaming, bright light illuminating her face. She was smiling with so much love and compassion in her eyes, telling me with her gentle and loving voice, "Do not cry. It's okay not to attend my funeral. Instead, I have come to you to say goodbye. I love you and I must go now."

I do not remember exactly all that she said. I just remember feeling so much love coming from her. She told me goodbye and the white light illuminating her beautiful face disappeared.

At that moment, I was in awe that she came to me. I felt so loved, but I knew no one would believe me, due to the fact that they did not believe I was old enough to attend her funeral. So I kept my experience to myself until more than twenty years later, when my aunt shared with me that her mom, which is my maternal grandmother, also came to her soon after she died, and she had a similar goodbye experience. We both were young, grieving with an abundance of love for her. God allowed us both to see a vision of her spirit before she left the earth. Her beautiful face and gentle voice were able to be seen and heard on the day of her funeral.

God was so generous to allow me to experience my grandmother's love for me and to nourish my broken heart. Feeling her overwhelming love soothed the pain in my broken heart at that moment.

God Gifts Us with Images to Warn Us

Anna, a newly reborn Christian, spent time with God on Sundays. By Tuesdays, her body was craving her old, sinful ways. Anna soon backslid from God and returned to her promiscuous lifestyle. One day, as she closed her eyes to rest, Anna felt something grab and restrain her body. She saw and felt herself being pulled down many feet under the earth. The farther down she went, the hotter it became. Looking down, she saw fire and demons. She screamed several times, "Jesus, save me!" She was then released and able to open her eyes. Feeling terrified and convicted, all at the same time, she got on her knees and repented to Jesus for backsliding.

Anna had underestimated the amounts of changes needed in her lifestyle to live a life serving God and ruling over sin. She soon made the necessary adjustments. She received deliverance from sexual strongholds, increased her intimate time with God, and started being a servant in the Kingdom of God. She now rules over sin.

God Gifts Us with the Ability to Create Our Own Images

We can create images of our dreams and goals. The energy from our thoughts, words, emotions, images, and actions works hard to move and make the necessary changes to manifest our visions into physical form.

First and foremost, every day, visualize God's Holy Angels guarding you and your family. Visualize thanking the Holy Angels for all their assistance. Visualize you and all those around you praising God, Jesus, and the Holy Spirit. Visualize peaceful and kind employers, neighbors, motorists, family, and friends. Visualize your goals and dreams.

After studying the different aspects of love for many years, I began to have thoughts about writing self-help books. The more thoughts I created, the more ideas and momentum were built within me to write books. I created images of people learning about God's love and feeling inspired to love. I have written two manuscripts. Once upon a time, my books were only an image within my mind.

The image you create should be in alignment with your beliefs you have about achieving your goals. For example, if your goal is to be physically fit, then visualize working out, lifting weights, eating healthy, and drinking adequate amounts of water. Then, apply action. If you do not like any of those things, ask yourself, "What do I like to do that helps me burn calories and eat less?" Do squats or lift dumbbells while streaming Christian movies. Every week, increase the amount of time working out. Lift a dumbbell for a few minutes a day. Imagine your body healthy. Get started from where you are right now! Start with a few images of your ideal weight, eating healthy, and working out, and slowly build a momentum of images, as if your goal is achieved right now.

I cannot stress the importance of you being accepting of and believing in the possibility of your images becoming reality. Start now and say, "Okay, this is what I will do today to move closer to my goal." In other words, if you have not recently exercised or done any physical activities, start slowly and do not set expectations to sign up for a marathon next week. If you weigh 300 pounds, do not expect in a few months to be 150 pounds. Yes, create images of you weighing 150 pounds and feeling as if you are 150 pounds; however, understand that along with faith, it takes time, patience, and work for your goal to manifest. In other words, do not be impatient with yourself. When we are anxious and our goals do not happen in the amount of time we desire, we may become discouraged and often go back to our old habits. So take baby steps.

We can create images to assist us with manifesting our dreams into existence. Spend a little time each day adding more details to your dreams. If it is a house, visualize the grass, the color of the house, the doorbell, or the floor type. Do not try to solve in your mind how you will purchase the home. Act and feel as if you have the home. Visualize going through your front door, as if it is happening in the present moment. Imagine you can smell the new carpet or wood. Your images, thoughts, and belief will create the opportunity for you to work toward getting your dream home. Be ready to do the work when the opportunity arrives. As you take the opportunity to do the work to manifest the home, soon the opportunity to purchase the home will arrive.

Look around you. Identify something you have that was initially a thought or a desire, and soon became images in your mind, and now it is here. How many times did you think about it before it manifested into the physical world? Everything around all of us was manifested using at least three out of the five communicators within our hearts and minds. When we visualize our dreams with belief and act as if the dream is presently here, a high level of energy forms within us, which allows us to work toward manifesting our goals. Various opportunities will move within our lives to help us accomplish our dreams.

God provides us with the ability to create images using faith, which includes energy. Those beautiful images we create using our hearts and minds can manifest within our lives when filled with faith and work. Are some of your images focused on helping others, spending time with God, and improving your mind, body, and soul? Do you believe the images you are creating will manifest? Some refer to it as luck or being in the right place at the right time, but our ability to create and manifest desires— by creating images using faith and applying work—is an another one of God's generous gifts to us.

Keep in mind that images that are not of the fruits of the Spirit also have energy and can move unproductive moments or setbacks in your direction. So keep your images productive and positive. God instructs us to keep our thoughts on truth, honor, justice, purity, love, and commendable and good things that are worthy of praising.

"And God spoke to Israel in a vision at night and said, 'Jacob! Jacob!'

'Here I am,' he replied."

GENESIS 46:2 NIV

"And behold, the glory of the God of Israel was there,

like the vision that I saw in the plain."

EZEKIEL 8:4

ENERGY IN ACTIONS

"And whatever you do, do it heartily, as to the Lord and not to men."

COLOSSIANS 3:23

Joan, a sales representative for a major health company, canceled her plans to hang out at the beach, and instead, went to work for a coworker because he was feeling ill. Although she felt disappointed about changing her plans, she did not let onto him of her feelings or act as if he were a burden. She responded with a gentle and cheerful attitude, happy to sow a good seed.

Unbeknown to Joan, her coworker's pain escalated. He went to the hospital and was told he had appendicitis. While she worked his shift, Joan sold an exceptionally large account that day. It raised her sales performance from below average to exceeding her employer's monthly goal. Joan told everyone she was so appreciative for God's blessings.

Such stories as Joan's happen more often than we realize. When Joan gave from the heart, out of her care for another, the energy from her generosity and selfless act circled around a lucrative opportunity. It raised her sales performance from below average to exceeding her employer's monthly goal. Joan gave up her time to help someone in need. To give from the heart, not expecting anything in return, can often bring a speedy return.

I highly recommend that whenever you apply action to do a job, cheerfully give your heart and mind to your performance. Give fruits-of-the-Spirit behaviors to your job functions. The outcome of your performance will always be beneficial to you.

Work, work, work. Yes, we must work, whether it's a nine-to-five job, self-employment, school, or spiritual growth for the body, soul, and spirit. The moon, the sun, trees, and animals work consistently, and we benefit significantly. Work is necessary to accomplish any extraordinary goal, such as using our spiritual gifts to win souls to Jesus Christ. Working provides opportunities to display our Christian character and influence souls to be redeemed by God. Satan instigates humans to gravitate to their sinful and selfish nature, instead of using their spiritual gifts for the Kingdom of God. Walking in the fruits of the Spirit empowers us to rule over our sinful and selfish nature and to stay woke to Satan's schemes to influence sin. The energy from fruits-of-the-Spirit behaviors helps to strengthen us to keep working hard and to do the right thing the right way.

Memorize Scriptures and Say Daily to Inspire You to Use Your Energy to Be Productive

"The soul of a lazy man desires, and has nothing; but the soul of the diligent shall be made rich." (Proverbs 13:4)

"For even when we were with you, we commanded you this: If anyone will not work, neither shall he eat. For we hear that there are some who walk among you in a disorderly manner, not working at all, but are busybodies. Now those who are such we command and exhort through our Lord Jesus Christ that they work in quietness and eat their own bread." (2 Thessalonians 3:10-12)

"I can do all things through Christ who
strengthens me." (Philippians 4:13)

"In all labor there is profit, but idle chatter leads only to poverty."
(Proverbs 14:23)

"Do all things without complaining and disputing, that you may become
blameless and harmless, children of God without fault in the midst of
a crooked and perverse generation, among whom you shine as lights in
the world." (Philippians 2:14-15)

"Therefore, whether you eat or drink, or whatever you do,
do all to the glory of God." (1 Corinthians 10:31)

Chapter Seven

APPLYING GOD'S EXTRAORDINARY ENERGY

L et us summarize how each day you can apply your thoughts, words, emotions, images, and actions—known as the five communicators—to express love to God the Father, the Son, the Holy Spirit, and Holy Angels. Reciprocating love to God keeps you connected to God's Kingdom. If you abide in God, all your needs will be supplied. Do you need healing? God heals. Do you need deliverance? God delivers. God is the greatest love you can ever experience.

EXPRESS LOVE TO GOD USING THE FIVE COMMUNICATORS

Images

Each day create images of spending sacred time in the mornings, afternoons, and at night. Give thanks and appreciation to God the

Father, Jesus Christ, the Holy Spirit and Holy Angels for the blessings you receive.

Thoughts
Every day memorize a scripture of God's expectations for you to love.

Words
Every day recite the scriptures you memorized and express verbally your love for God and the Kingdom of God.

Emotions
Rejoice and feel appreciation for God's generosity.

Actions
Show appreciation to God, Jesus, and the Holy Spirit through praise, worship, prayer, reading your Bible, conversation, and resonating loving behaviors within all your encounters (with people, animals, plants, and the environment) throughout the day. Each day identify one of God's creations that you utilize and how that creation expresses love to you. For example, experts say that pineapples are packed with nutrients, enzymes, and antioxidants that can help fight inflammation and disease.

EXPRESS SELF-LOVE USING THE FIVE COMMUNICATORS

Images
Create images of your short- and long-term goals. Believe, act, and feel as if your goals have already been accomplished.

Thoughts
Maintain positive thoughts on what you see, feel, taste, smell, and hear as much as possible.

Words

Say words of encouragement about your body and mind, your goals, and your relationships.

Emotions

Apply steps to turn on your feel-good chemicals. (Refer to the chapter *Joy* for examples.)

Actions

Give yourself affirmations each day for the strength to stay present, eat healthy, and exercise, or complete some form of mobility daily, such as clean the house or car, wash and fold clothes, or rake the yard. Each morning, say the following affirmation: "I will experience an abundance of happiness today."

EXPRESS LOVE TO OTHERS USING THE FIVE COMMUNICATORS

Thoughts

Discover and think about others accomplishing their goals: "Therefore love the stranger, for you were strangers in the land of Egypt." (Deuteronomy 10:19)

Words

Speak kind, gentle, and peaceful words to others.

Emotions

Feel a sense of appreciation, joy, and happiness for others.

Images

Create images of others accomplishing their goals. Create images of ways God can use you to be a blessing to them.

Actions

Work toward resolutions, agreements, and acceptance of each other's goals: "For we do not wrestle against flesh and blood, but against principalities, against powers, against the rulers of the darkness of this age, against spiritual hosts of wickedness in the heavenly places." (Ephesians 6:12)

Part Three

UNDERSTANDING GOD'S EXTRAORDINARY RULE OVER SIN

Chapter Eight

RULE OVER SIN: AN EXTRAORDINARY GIFT FROM GOD

"Therefore do not let sin reign in your mortal body, that you should obey it in

its lusts. And do not present your members as instruments of unrighteousness

to sin, but present yourselves to God as being alive from the dead, and your members

as instruments of righteousness to God."

ROMANS 6:12-13

There will come a time when Jesus Christ's faithful followers will be surrounded with all that is pure, loving, joyful, and righteous. There will be no more tears, lies, broken hearts, loneliness, pain, poverty, addiction, stealing, or killing. There will be no more interference from Satan.

However, at this present time, Satan and his demons roam the earth, tempting humans to sin. The good news is that Jesus Christ has taught His followers how to rule over sin. The Holy Spirit and armored Holy Angels can and will help us. Yes, in Jesus' name, through the power of the Holy Spirit, we are empowered to rule over sin and spread righteous love.

Satan is aware that Jesus' sacrifice on the cross has given us, reborn Christians, an inheritance of power to rule over sin, heal sickness, break curses, and win souls to Christ. Satan knows the Kingdom of God is more powerful than Satan's tribe, and the only way for Satan to form war against humans is through lies, manipulating and baiting humans to sin, and enslaving them to be ruled by sin.

Humans are equipped to overpower Satan's kingdom. We can faithfully work for God. We are not sinless, but we are able to rule over sin. Jesus Christ was the only one on earth who was always good and never sinned.

WHAT RULES INSIDE OF YOU?

> *"Jesus answered them, 'Most assuredly,*
> *I say to you, whoever commits sin is a slave of sin.'"*
>
> JOHN 8:34

Janice and her boyfriend Donald, with whom she shares an apartment, are doing better. Janice recently received a pay increase and Donald started a new job. They are parents of twin boys and Janice's postpartum depression was far behind her. The future looked promising. She often pondered about getting married, joining a church, and getting involved in church-related activities. However, she currently worked six days a week to cover her boyfriend's recent unemployment.

Janice settled her pondering by telling herself that once she paid off a few bills and ceased working overtime, both she and her kids would be able to attend church. As time went on, her working overtime ended, but she still did not attend any church. There was always an excuse. As far as Donald was concerned, he was content with his life and did not have any interest in going to church. Donald's focus was on making money for his family, watching sports, and socially drinking.

A few years passed, and Donald's focus changed.

He began to have an affair with a woman named Arika. Unbeknown to Donald, Arika had multiple problems housed within her body, including depression, suicide, sexual immorality, and other spirits from Arika's former lovers and *their* lovers. Not to mention the problems caused by the demons from Donald's affair with her.

Arika had been witnessed to by a Christian. She rejected the invitation and continued her sinful lifestyle, relying solely on her own strength and medicine to get rid of the migraines, suppress the insomnia, and numb the depression and negative thoughts.

I am not saying that all health problems stem from demons. Absolutely not. There are other ways to develop health problems without Satan's involvement. However, sexual sin is a sin against the body; therefore, it opens a gateway for demons to attack the body. I am an advocate for medicine and a licensed expert's assistance for treatment. However, renouncing demons in the name of Jesus Christ with the power of the Holy Spirit, turning away from sin, praying, and fasting is the way to ultimate deliverance and healing.

Her choice of remedy did not get rid of her problems. It temporarily helped her function while demons assaulted her. Arika's reaction to the excessive feeling of sexual arousal was to be promiscuous. She felt guilty that some of her lovers had families, but her will to do the right thing was weakened, because she unknowingly released her energy over to Satan through actively sinning. This is one of the reasons it feels tremendously difficult (but not impossible) to stop. Satan had legally weakened her energy and raised enormous desires for her sexual sins. Although she succumbed to Satan's stronghold, she still had the energy and free will to successfully resist. But it would be extremely difficult to achieve without calling on the Kingdom of God for help. She would be more at risk to backslide to her sinful nature without the Kingdom of God's assistance. However, by praying, fasting, and renouncing in Jesus Christ's name with the power of the Holy Spirit, it is possible for her to be delivered and regain her power expeditiously.

Janice, like Arika, had her own demons and here came more, being sexually transmitted through David. Arika's spirit of depression, along with other demons, gained access into Janice's body through David going back and forth sexually between both women. This almost led Janice to her fatality. The demons from Arika began to target Janice's vulnerable areas. They resurfaced within her what felt like postpartum depression, but there was no new birth. Janice became baffled about the feeling of overwhelming sadness that was happening for no apparent reason. Things had been going well.

Janice eventually went to the doctor and was prescribed medication. She soon stopped taking the pills because of the side effects. The horrendous flood of sadness returned. She could not sleep at night. Donald staying out more frequently at night did not help. When she took sleeping pills to get some rest, she had dreams that Donald was having affairs. She had nightmares of snakes and scorpions crawling in her bed. When she awakened, she accused him of cheating. They started arguing and fighting frequently. He accused her of being crazy. She started calling out from her job, too lifeless to get up in the morning.

This went on for months, until she felt as if she could not take another breath. She drank an entire bottle of liquor and passed out. Janice awakened to taunting thoughts to end her life. She described her mental state as feeling as if she had almost no energy to fight for her life. Janice went into the medicine cabinet and opened a bottle of pills. She placed the entire bottle of pills in her mouth.

The twins would be devastated, finding me dead. Overwhelmed with grief that Mommy did not fight to be there for them, Janice thought, and out of love for the twins, she spit the pills out of her mouth.

Her fate in almost facing death terrified Janice. She made an appointment to receive a different type of prescribed medicine for her feelings of despair and sadness.

During her session, Janice's doctor asked if she had a support system. Janice thought about it. That was her turning point. Janice thought of her late grandmother, who was a God-fearing woman and always had lots of support from her church. The doctor's questions and Janice's recollection of her grandmother being surrounded by loving church members motivated Janice.

She and her children joined a Bible-based church and became born-again Christians. She joined the Bible study group. They had potlucks and prayed together. Janice established a good support system with a few church members. Her late grandmother had advised her to always have a good support system. Because in life, at one time or another, everyone experiences a fall-down or setback, and your support team can help you and you can help them.

Donald confessed to what was apparent: his affair. Janice eventually left Donald. Instead of fighting and binge-drinking, Janice took that pain and turned to Jesus. Janice started praying and reading several chapters in her Bible every time her heart ached about the breakup of her family and every night before she went to bed. Her broken heart healed, and her bad dreams ended.

One morning, she woke up and felt a burst of energy. The first thing she would normally do in the morning was take her antidepressant pill, but instead, she read her Bible and prayed. This soon became her new routine. She began to feel happy again. Her doctor authorized her to stop taking the prescribed medicine.

The love for her children strengthened Janice's will to live.

Choose the road of love! It conquers a multitude of Satan's schemes to destroy your life.

DO YOU HAVE A GOOD SUPPORT SYSTEM?

Are you listening to the Holy Spirit or Satan? Can you hear the Holy Spirit? Are Satan and unclean spirits distracting you?

Sometimes, when something is wrong with us, it is not what is wrong with *us*, but *who* is within us. Develop a good support system. A Christian support team can be a few righteous and reliable people, who absolutely love God and support one another to stay strong in their relationship with Jesus Christ and help one another in times of need. They regularly have Bible study, pray, and fellowship together. They often provide daily prayer, kind words, and gifts to each other during times of sorrow, which can contribute to a speedy recovery.

We are not sinless, so demons can resurface time and time again. However, the sinner can resist demons. The consistency of resisting the temptation will require demons to flee.

As you resist sin, turn toward loving others during the time you would normally sin. Each time we partake in certain sins, we are harming our souls by losing energy, enslaving our will, and creating a cobweb of entrapment to Satan. The sinful acts influence a flood of thoughts, words, emotions, images, and actions that lead us in the opposite direction of the Kingdom of God, clouding one's judgement. This is another reason why it is so important to repent, forgive, and love daily.

Satan sends an active sinner thoughts, words, emotions, and images that become clearer and stronger within the sinner, who then begins to feel connected, as one, to the sin. The road toward enslavement becomes wider. The soul's communication to its spirit becomes weaker, impairing one's ability to interpret righteous communication and warnings. It is like a cell phone losing its signal bars. The deeper the soul's heart and mind are enthralled with sin, the less cell phone signal bars the soul's body has available to hear, interpret, and speak to the soul's spirit, who receives information from God's Kingdom. The soul's communication to its spirit weakens so much that soon the soul is completely distracted by Satan's systematic strategy. The active sinner becomes very vulnerable to clearly receiving communication from demons in the form of sinful thoughts, words, emotions, images, and encounters.

Not all sinful thoughts, images, words, and emotions come from demons; they also come from people. Stay conscious and remember that Satan's ultimate target is to kill the body, steal the soul, and destroy the opportunity for everlasting life with God and His Kingdom. Unfortunately, an unbeliever of Christ, who is unrepentant and unforgiving, often does not accept the truth until the soul completely exits (through death) the physical body. While the sinner is in Hell, Satan then reveals to the sinner how he lied and tricked them to destroy their opportunity for everlasting life with God.

Come on and outsmart Satan. Continue to renounce the temptation and quote scriptures until you feel the temptation subsiding.

Jealousy, anger, laziness, and fear are common doors for demons to come through and into you. When feeling those emotions, call out in the name of Jesus with the power of the Holy Spirit for the spirits to leave.

Repent. Ask for forgiveness. Proceed to do the opposite of your attack. For example, when you experience jealousy, pray and speak blessings toward your target. Then, move your thoughts onto something that makes you happy. Do activities that build your self-esteem. Listen to a righteous, uplifting song; memorize and say scriptures about happiness; and visualize things that make you happy. Do these things until you feel relief and happiness.

Below are some strategies to rule over sin and defeat sin enslavement.

DO THE FOLLOWING TO CLEANSE YOUR SOUL OF SINS

1. **Repent.** Admit to God your sins. Ask God to remove the strongholds of sins. Ask for forgiveness. Ask God to forgive you and your family members who committed sins which may have brought upon a generational curse. For example, if there is a generational spirit of adultery within the family because of repeated adulterous sins, ask God to forgive everyone. Really be sincere.

2. **Renounce the Unclean Spirits**. Sins bring "unclean spirits," or demons, within your life. For example, to renounce, say, "In the name of Jesus with the power of the Holy Spirit, I command you, spirit of jealousy, to come out of me and not return." Each time the urge to sin reappears, renounce in the name of Jesus with the power of the Holy Spirit to rid all demons. Whenever they return, renounce again. Renounce daily if necessary.

3. **Renew the Mind.** If you are renewing your mind and turning away from lustful thoughts, do the following for a few days:

Refrain from all secular television, social media, and secular music (always refrain), and distance yourself from those you feel lust toward. When a thought surfaces for you to backslide, rebuke those thoughts and feelings. However, if you are not on guard and accidently entertain a lustful thought, immediately repent. Stay busy doing the following, or similar, actions: fellowship, write, read, pray, go to Bible study, do puzzles, paint. Gradually resume *only* viewing acceptable G-rated content. Limit social media to the following: YouTube videos of sermons; G-rated movies and shows; Christian movies, songs, and comedy; and Christians' testimonies of becoming believers in Christ. If the person you feel lust toward isn't someone you are engaged to or intend to marry, remove yourself from being around that individual you feel lust toward until you rule over that sin by ceasing lustful thoughts and feelings toward them. Replace those thoughts and feelings with godly thoughts about something else. If it is your soon-to-be fiancé that you're lusting, always have people around the both of you until that big day. Ask elders to pray for you. Refrain from physical contact; however, a quick hug or an innocent smack on the cheek for greetings and departures, at times, may be safe. Do not be alone with each other until that wedding day. Interact in settings that are around others, such as church, Christian concerts, couple's meetings with a therapist, parks, restaurants, the library, your home when others are there, volunteering events at the Humane Society, cooking classes, or sports games with other couples. These are all ideal places.

READING THE BIBLE DAILY TO POSITIVELY RENEW YOUR MIND

As you read the stories of the Bible, think about the positive message. Doing so will help replace your flesh desires. For example, read about Paul communicating to the Corinthians, Philippians, and many others, out of faithfulness and deep love. Do so at a time you may normally snack on junk food or talk on the phone to gossip; instead, read a chapter in your Bible. Do this daily, and soon it will become a habit. Christians have successfully replaced poor habits with experiencing God's perfect love by reading the Bible daily.

As you read and imagine the stories of Jesus' healing, forgiveness, and acceptance, you begin to feel God's love. Fear dissipates and love begins to illuminate within you. Soon, a higher level of appreciation for God develops, as you spend time reading about God's love for us. You begin to learn and understand His enormous level of love and intelligence. You feel honored and inspired to spend time with God. Seeking to retain communication from God, a sense of humility is adopted.

FASTING

(Inquire with your physician regarding fasting.)

Regularly fasting can strengthen the soul to walk in the fruits of the Spirit, control the flesh, and renounce demons. Each time you say no to the flesh desires, you are strengthening your spirit and weakening your flesh. Give yourself credit, even for the smallest resistance. Whether it's twelve hours or twelve days of fasting from junk food, TV, social media, or immoral sex, you are strengthening your spirit and your will and weakening your flesh. This is *awesome*. Therefore, when a temptation surfaces within your life, the strength to resist the flesh is developed, which creates more opportunities to win against your temptation and rule over sin.

PRAISE AND WORSHIP DAILY

This is an opportunity to express genuine love and appreciation to God the Father, Jesus, and the Holy Spirit. Praising God is a tremendous way to express gratitude to God. For example, when a young Christian praises God on her nature walks, she expresses gratefulness for the beautiful trees, animals, clean air, insects, a safe walk, and her freedom.

PRAY THROUGHOUT THE DAY

Praying without ceasing daily is a powerful way to stay connected to the Father, the Son, the Holy Spirit, and Holy Angels. Schedule a time to pray for others and the self. When leaders made decisions without first consulting God, such as Joshua and others in the Bible, they caused themselves unnecessary grief and hardship. However, when they consulted God and followed His will, they experienced victory time and time again.

Do not be anxious about anything, but pray and consult God about everything before you decide. When David, Elijah, Elisha, and other followers consulted God and complied, God victoriously answered their prayers.

WALK IN THE FRUITS OF THE SPIRIT

As we nourish our souls daily with these steps, our souls strengthen and become more apt to receive, retain, and process information received from our spirits, which receive information from the Holy Spirit. Walking in the fruits of the Spirit daily is like eating an adequate amount of healthy food, drinking water, exercising, getting proper rest, and refraining from unhealthy behaviors. The fruits-of-the-Spirit behaviors are love, joy, peace, patience, kindness, goodness, faithfulness, gentleness, and self-control. Such habits strengthen and refuel the physical body. In return, the physical body feels good, energized, and refueled continuously. Plant seeds of being loving, joyful, peaceful, patient, kind, good, faithful, gentle, and self-controlled daily, and good people, such as honest mechanics, honest contractors, and good Samaritans, will sprout up all around you.

INTERCESSORY PRAYER

When you are fighting a temptation, request other Christians, who may not have the same struggle as yourself, to pray for you. It is okay to be vulnerable with the believers of Jesus Christ. Requesting intercessory prayer is a powerful resource to receive from one another, especially during challenging times.

AWARENESS OF GOD'S EXTRAORDINARY LOVE AND POWER

Be cognitive of all the extraordinary love and power you possess through God the Father, Jesus Christ the Son, the Holy Spirit, and Holy Angels. Jesus lovingly provides us His grace. When Jesus returned to Heaven, God sent the comforter, who is the Holy Spirit.

"But the Helper, the Holy Spirit, whom the Father will send in My name, He will teach you all things, and bring to your remembrance all things that I said to you."
JOHN 14:26

In the name of Jesus, ask the Holy Spirit to always bless you with power and a heart to rule over sin. The Holy Spirit can send thoughts and sounds to us. The Holy Spirit can comfort and protect us. Ask the Holy Spirit to always remind you how to love in all you do.

Ask the Holy Spirit to teach you all that is prevalent for you to learn to conquer demons. Ask the Holy Spirit to expose any ungodly intent from others toward you and to protect you.

FORGIVENESS

Forgive others. Forgive yourself for anything you feel conviction and renounce relevant unclean spirits by saying, "In the name of Jesus Christ with the power of the Holy Spirit, I command you, spirit of guilt, to come out of me and flee." If the guilty thoughts or feelings return, renounce the demon again. Change whatever you are doing or thinking to involve righteous love. Demons hate godly love. Everyone will experience hurt, because we have a sinful nature, but part of that journey is forgiving, learning from our mistakes, and moving toward love.

Who do you need to forgive?

Forgiveness is a daily act we exercise, which helps keep us connected to God and far away from Satan. Forgive daily the people who offend you. Write down their names and ask the Holy Spirit and Holy Angels to help you forgive. Repent daily and ask the Holy Spirit to help you walk in the fruits of the Spirit each day.

Chapter Nine

SEEK THE HOLY SPIRIT

The Holy Spirit is readily available to comfort, instruct, and guide us throughout our journeys on earth. Believers can rule over sin through the power of the Holy Spirit.

HER SPIRITUAL GIFT COULD HAVE LED MORE SOULS TO JESUS CHRIST

I was in my early twenties when I met a woman named Thelma. She appeared to be in her sixties. Thelma was born with the gift to see into the spiritual world. She could see and hear what she believed to be deceased people, who were highly active in humans' lives. These deceased people would provide her information about people's livelihoods. They sent thoughts to humans, and sometimes the receiver would believe it was their own thought or idea. Some even believed God was talking to them. They influenced a lot of people. Thelma believed her information from them helped people. She referred to them as her spirit guides. She told me, when she was young, she joined a church to help people. She eventually stopped going to church. She concluded church and prophesying for the church was not required or necessary in life.

I wish I would have inquired about how she came to such a conclusion. To make such a remark. I am convinced those spirit guides (demons) battled with the church to keep Thelma in darkness. She did not see anything wrong in consulting these familiar spirit guides, instead of consulting the Holy Spirit. I do not know if her former church, or Thelma herself, believed in the Holy Spirit. The Holy Spirit will always respect our God-given free will. Therefore, the Holy Spirit most likely, grievously, allowed Thelma's will.

After leaving church, Thelma started her own clairvoyant classes, teaching her students how to see and talk to demons. By the time she and I crossed paths in life, Thelma had retired from teaching clairvoyant classes. This was fortunate for my friend and me, because we would have naively taken the class and opened a dimension that was even further away from the truth than where we currently were. This would have created more problems for myself, as I did not know Jesus Christ at that time.

Upon reflection, I now realize that through her free will, her thoughts and sounds were being ruled by Satan. Thelma used her gifts to teach classes that ultimately gave demons access to keep a lot of souls in darkness, instead of using her gifts to win souls to Christ and edify the church.

IN AN IRONIC TWIST

When I met Thelma, she could have led me down the same path she led her former students. Instead, in an ironic twist, she helped direct me down another path, which led me to love. To God. To Jesus.

She had retired from teaching clairvoyant classes on how to consult spirit guides (demons), but she continued to consult demons for her clients. I refer to the spirit guides as demons because they distracted vulnerable people from seeking Jesus, and instead, grew dependent upon them.

The day before I met Thelma, I was really broken and felt like I wanted to end my life. I cried out, and said, "God, are you real? If so, please let me know. Why are we here? Please, help me. I don't have the strength to go on."

At that time, I was deeply hurting, confused, and wanted to know the truth about my existence on earth. I doubted God existed. I felt so tortured and empty inside.

The day that I met Thelma, she told me that I am my worst enemy (negative) and my future looked just as gloomy as my present. She explained to me what she saw to come to such a conclusion.

Feeling defeated and baffled, I asked, "How do I change my direction?"

Instead of her offering for me to return for a session to help me, she said, "Go to God for help. I don't know. Ask God for help. Read positive books." I listened with astonishment, not because she knew things about me, but because she was a clairvoyant and acted more like an ambassador for God. She didn't allow her spirit guides to help me, or invite me to another session.

I thought about my plea to God, wanting to know if God was real and crying to God to help me get out of a tortured and empty place. I felt that

God caused an intervention from Thelma's spirit guides, because prior to this, I desperately pleaded to God to know the truth and I sincerely wanted help from God to live accordingly. I appreciated Thelma for allowing herself to be used to refer me to God, instead of to her demons. Thelma referring me to God helped lead me down the path of learning how to be positive and how to love. I later joined a good Bible-based church and became a reborn Christian. I believe my sincere and desperate plea to God helped to will an intervention against Thelma and her spirit guides' normal routine.

I strongly advise everyone not to consult psychics, clairvoyants, mediums, or those who are similar. Yes, it is a sin. It is one of the easiest points of access for demons to enter into you. Demons are there when you are having a reading and invite themselves into your lives. If you have done so in the past, confess your sins, ask God for forgiveness, and renounce all demons in Jesus' name with the power of the Holy Spirit. God is the Creator and has all the answers and resources we need. Seek the Father of Jesus Christ. Seek a good Bible-based church to help you.

ARE YOU USING YOUR EXTRAORDINARY SPIRITUAL GIFTS?

What are your spiritual gifts? Are you using them to lead people to Jesus Christ, our Lord and Savior?

Listening to the Holy Spirit can help us discover our extraordinary spiritual gifts, such as the gift of healing, gift of discernment, gift of counsel, gift of prophesying, and more. These gifts lead one to a fulfilling life, serving in the Kingdom of God and ruling over sin. Satan will try to sway a person to use their spiritual gifts in ungodly ways; however, if a

Christian abides closely with the Holy Spirit, his or her spiritual gifts can be used immeasurably in the Kingdom of God.

GIVE THANKS TO THE HOLY SPIRIT

"Or do you not know that your body is the temple of the Holy Spirit who is in you, whom you have from God, and you are not your own?"

1 CORINTHIANS 6:19

When a Christian abides with the Holy Spirit, the ability to walk in the fruits of the Spirit, which Galatians 5:22-23 says, "But the fruit of the Spirit is love, joy, peace, longsuffering, kindness, goodness, faithfulness, gentleness, self-control" becomes possible through the power of the Holy Spirit.

"I say then: Walk in the Spirit, and you shall not fulfill the lust of the flesh."

GALATIANS 5:16

Demons must flee when we repeatedly say no to sin and choose to walk in the Spirit. As we abide in the Holy Spirit, we are empowered with self-control to not be ruled by fleshly behaviors, such as those listed in Galatians 5:19-21: "Now the works of the flesh are evident, which are: adultery, fornication, uncleanness, lewdness, idolatry, sorcery, hatred, contentions, jealousies, outbursts of wrath, selfish ambitions, dissensions, heresies, envy, murders, drunkenness, revelries, and the like; of which I tell you beforehand, just as I also told you in time past, that those who practice such things will not inherit the kingdom of God."

The Holy Spirit will comfort you in all of your steps.

"But the Helper, the Holy Spirit, whom the Father will send in My name, He will teach you all things, and bring to your remembrance all things that I said to you."

JOHN 14:26

The more you resist sin and spend time in prayer, communication from the Holy Spirit will become clearer and you will be able to discern which thoughts are sent by Satan.

Utilize your power given by the Holy Spirit to speak your request into existence. For example, there was a time when I was struggling to overcome the temptation of returning to a toxic relationship. I said, "In the name of Jesus Christ with the power of the Holy Spirit, I renounce you, spirit of lust, spirit of loneliness. Come out of my body." I renounced multiple times and proceeded to do something that was the opposite of what Satan was tempting me to do in that moment. I went on an outing with my friends and embraced every moment with them.

Chapter Ten

BE ON GUARD OF SATAN'S TACTICS

"Behold, I send you out as sheep in the midst of wolves.
Therefore be wise as serpents and harmless as doves."

MATTHEW 10:16

Every day, there are demons assigned from Satan's evil kingdom to instigate as many humans as possible to sin. But we, the followers of Jesus Christ, can defeat Satan and rule over sin. Satan is the king of lies, manipulation, and tricks. Satan hates humans and betrays even those who may possibly worship and idolize him, such as witches, Satanists, and Wiccans. They are oblivious of his hate toward them because he is a master manipulator, deceiver, and trickster.

Satan does not want humans to know that every single day we should sincerely love, repent, forgive, and be courageous to love with our entire hearts and minds. I do mean sincerely.

This is exceptionally beneficial for you. Regardless of how small your encounters appear—whether it's your dog doing an accident on your new floor or a motorist tailgating you—if you felt anything outside of the fruits of the Spirit during the encounter, please repent. If you felt patience and understanding of your dog's accident, then excellent. We all have demons within our lives. However, either through the self or from a disciple, deliverance and consistent reciprocation of love, repentance, forgiveness, and the courage to extend godly love in all our encounters can help keep demons powerless in our lives. If the person you encounter is displaying non-loving behaviors, pray for a peaceful interaction with them, and when necessary, plea the blood of Jesus with the power of the Holy Spirit, renouncing those demons within that individual.

Demons are not able to reside in humans' hearts and minds, where godly love resides. For example, the very second you lie or gossip, here comes a demon. We are not perfect and we all sin. Simply a judgmental thought (adults' minds house thousands of thoughts a day) is a sin and invites demons within your life. When your heart and mind change with the intent to love everyone, demons start to leave. For example, if you choose to be patient when you are tempted to be impatient, the demons that influence impatience must leave. Just keep resisting. If you choose to forgive, instead of holding a grudge, demons must leave. If you choose to maintain self-control, instead of giving in to an unhealthy habit, demons must leave. The fruits-of-the-Spirit actions peel away Satan's blindfolds and become authentic within you. But when you fall short and sin—please, I beg you—please repent, and when applicable, forgive others. Walk with courage. Granted, it is incredibly challenging to walk in the fruits-of-the-Spirit during a conflict. Pray and ask for the Holy Spirit's assistance as soon as you recognize you may not be resolving the conflict with the fruits-of-the-Spirit behavior.

Love. I mean, *love!* Love! Love as many people and animals as often as possible. This is the greatest way to get rid of demons, rule over sin, heal, and experience love. Satan's other main strategies are to influence nonproductive habits, entertain sinful and negative thoughts, promote fear instead of courage, and convince you not to fulfill your commitments and responsibilities. I will share why it's necessary to develop strategies in these areas of your life to remain on guard of Satan's tactics.

Write down your behaviors. Simply not being on guard can lead you down a road of sin enslavement. Demons know a lot about humans. They study humans to learn how they can influence us to sin. An idle mind is a major attraction for demons to communicate suggestions, which can eventually lead to a road of distractions, losses, problems, or possibly destruction.

Learn what weapons Satan uses to influence you to succumb to certain sins. If you are unsure, ask the Holy Spirit to help you become aware of your sins. For example, a long time ago, at a time when I was often feeling irritable and unbeknown to suppressed anger, one of my friends dreamed about me being angry. She dreamed that I was holding a bag full of apples while arguing with another friend. Each time I argued, an apple dropped out of my bag and rolled away. Before she awakened, only a few apples remained.

During that same time, I also dreamed of me being angry at people or them being angry with me. After I awakened from my dream that day, although I strived to be kind, the people around me appeared to be one step from wanting to argue.

Thinking back, I concluded my inappropriate anger was possibly suppressed within me. I had experienced a fair amount of loss, for which I harbored inappropriate resentment. I ignored how I felt and directed my attention on other things, instead of addressing my inappropriate anger. My friend and our prophetic dreams provided me with a revelation. I began to renounce, repent, and ask for forgiveness. I was angry, and it was not righteous anger, because it was not out of love, mercy, or justice.

"Then Jesus went into the temple of God and drove out all of those
who bought and sold in the temple, and overturned the tables of the money
changers and the seats of those who sold doves."
MATTHEW 21:12

My anger had stemmed from pride and jealousy. I decided to let go of my resentment and use my thoughts and words to send love to my competitor at work.

The angry dreams ended, and the mood in my environment became pleasant. Had I ignored the ungodly type of anger within me, the spirit of anger would have continued to seethe within and around me, awaiting its opportunity to instigate an explosion.

DEVELOP POWERFUL HABITS

"Set your mind on things above, not on things on the earth."
COLOSSIANS 3:2

The subconscious mind does a great work for us. It stores our experiences, thoughts, and habits. The subconscious mind allows us to feel a sense of comfort as we go about our routines.

Recall a time where you were driving your usual route home and when you arrived, you said, "I do not remember driving home." It is common for the subconscious to do our habits, as we can sometimes drift off and daydream or reminisce, instead of being in the present moment. Another example is when we have recurring emotions resurface throughout the day and our reaction is normally a routine response. When a person feels stressed or frustrated, some positive habits we can develop are to pray, exercise, read the Bible and positive books, praise and worship God, say affirmations, help others, clean things, dance, sing, play, and other actions. Some negative habits we may have formed to feel better are to eat, gossip, smoke, pop a pill, get drunk, or other similar behaviors. All of these divert from those unpleasant emotions and help us get into a state of temporary comfort. The subconscious mind does its job by reminding us to do our habits, as well as provide us with a feeling of comfort when we do them, regardless of if our habits are healthy or detrimental. Its job is to *remind* us to do the habit we've formed.

Discomforting emotions may surface when we initially change our habits. An example of discomfort might be coming home to watch a movie, but the cable is out; the apartment maintenance has temporarily turned off your water to do some work at a time when you would normally brush your teeth, brew coffee, or take a shower; or your air conditioner stops working in 90-degree weather. Discomfort is also felt when you initially stop smoking or drinking, and initially start exercising or eating healthy. Thankfully, the discomfort subsides after we become consistent in doing our new routines. If it's a sinful habit, the discomfort will be enormous, and I recommend taking steps such as repentance and casting out demons (which is described within this book). The consistency of your new routine will soon cause the subconscious mind to recognize your new routine as a new habit, which might have been to no longer smoke or drink and begin to exercise and eat healthy. Time and consistency will bring about new habits and feelings of comfort. Soon, your new behaviors, such as exercising, praying, and eating healthy, among others, will feel as effortless as waking up each morning.

Remember to take small steps each day when forming new, healthy habits. Move slow. During your free time, maintain for at least two minutes the images and thoughts of things you do that bring upon happiness and motivation within you. Repetitive, happy thoughts will cause the memory to resurface thoughts and images that turn on your happy feelings, along with much energy, motivating you to do those things. Repetitive images and thoughts of your goals and feelings, as if you are getting ready to accomplish your goal before the sunset, will give you repetitive motivation to work toward your goal.

Avoid behaviors associated with alcohol, drugs, sexually immorality, and others that can similarly alter your thoughts. Be careful of too much idle time and maintain positive habits that accommodate your relationship to the Kingdom of God. Satan will attempt to influence Christians to go back to bad habits, which can distract Christians from focusing on the Kingdom of God.

RENEWED LIFE

"And do not be conformed to this world, but be transformed by the renewing of your mind, that you may prove what is that good and acceptable and perfect will of God."
ROMANS 12:2

When Jana was addicted to drugs, she felt enslaved to her addictions. Her drug addiction chose when and what she did and how often. Her addiction led to the loss of family, loss of multiple jobs, going to jail, being homeless, getting into fights, and promiscuous behavior. Letting go of her addictions allowed her to be released from Satan's tormenting imprisonment and to build a new life in Christ.

Jana has become a Christian and a fitness trainer, who eats healthy most days. She treats herself to a sugary and fatty meal two times a week. Her motto is to not eat unhealthy foods or repeat any unhealthy habit, like sleeping in, being idle, et cetera, for more than two consecutive days. She says it's easier to not be controlled by, or form, a bad habit if it's not done often or consecutively. She also formed the habits to work out four times a week, intermittent fast at night, and eat healthy five days a week.

During those disciplined times, she feels empowered and strong enough to do the things that inspire her to love, like reading her Bible, giving praise and worship, et cetera. Jana is not sinless, but she rules over sin by waking up every day, initiating walking in the Spirit, and serving Jesus Christ.

DO THE RIGHT THING THE RIGHT WAY

In Genesis 4, Abel demonstrated obedience and faithfulness to God by bringing God the fat portions from some of the firstborn of his flock. God was pleased with Abel and his offering. His brother Cain did not do the same. Cain possibly picked over some crops to give as an offering to God. Therefore, Cain and his offering were not accepted.

The rejection made Cain terribly angry. God spoke to Cain about being upset and told Cain he would also be accepted if he did what was right. God also warned Cain that if he did what was not right, sin would be at his door, anxious to take control over him. Cain must not be subdued by sin, but instead rule over it. Unfortunately, Cain allowed sin to rule within him, and he killed his brother.

This story is an example of allowing our sinful nature to lead us away from God and into Satan's bondages. Cain's sinful behavior led him to feel rejected, rageful, and jealous. Those emotions must have felt tormenting, lowering his energy to an ungodly level where demons roam. It is my opinion that Satan influenced Cain by sending thoughts to stir those tormenting feelings, which influenced Cain to continue to sin. Unfortunately, Cain took the bait. God provided Cain an opportunity to repent and govern over sin, just as we are given chances.

Cain had an opportunity to subdue sin and govern over sin; he could have made right his wrong by repenting and giving the best portions of his crops. He needed to ask God for strength and a heart to be faithful. And he needed to ask God for strength to control his ungodly thoughts. All sinful thoughts do not come from demons; humans have a sinful nature. Cain may have had a greedy, sinful nature. When acted upon, Satan and his demons had legal rights to step in and instigate more sin, sending more sinful thoughts and urges. However, Cain had free will to resist those thoughts and urges, and if resisted, Satan must flee.

ELIMINATE FEAR

Waking up after experiencing one of my "witch-on-the-back" encounters, I immediately thought about what I saw while attempting to wake. I saw a spirit with an enormous amount of energy, with the looks and feel of a horrifying tornado. It was trying to pull me farther into the spiritual world; yet by using a lot of energy, I instinctively resisted and awakened, opening my eyes. As I became fully alert, I heard and felt a strong force go through me and exit out of my body. Amazed and scared at the same time, I thought, *As strong as that demon felt on me, it did not overpower my God-given strength, especially after I had fully awakened.* This means humans have extremely powerful, God-given energy.

118

I realized when we set our minds and hearts on something, even with a little faith, we literally can move our goals to us at a speed and intensity far greater than a tornado in the spiritual world. With consistent work, our goals will manifest in the physical world. Believe and consistently work toward your goal almost daily, whether it is ruling over a temptation or taking a college course. The energy that comes from your faith is greater than the energy from demons.

Renounce fear! Whenever you experience anxiety or fear, say, "In the name of Jesus with power of the Holy Spirit, I renounce you, spirit of fear. Leave, now!" Call out Jesus' name numerous times. Say it until you feel better.

Love! Love! Love righteously! Demons hate love and roam in the energy released from fear, hate, immoral sex, and anger. The more you walk in the fruits of the Spirit, the more powerful you become.

For God gave us not the spirit of fear, but of power, love, and self-control.

REMAIN POSITIVE

Allow edifying words to be stored in your memory, which is like always having medicine on hand. For example, I had a fear of doing a particular medical exam that lasted about twenty minutes. I asked my daughter to be in the exam room to comfort me. However, my fears did not subside as we entered the room. My heart was beating rapidly. My daughter began to pray for me as the nurse went over the procedure with me and during the exam. I recited the scripture, Isaiah 26:3, during the entire exam, which allowed me to feel God was with me and in control.

Chapter Eleven

HELL

*"And the smoke of their torment ascends forever and ever; and they
have no rest day and night, who worship the beast and his image, and
whoever receives the mark of his name."*

REVELATION 14:11

Wow! Where do I begin? God's love for us is so visible. Have you thought about how bad eternal life would be without God?

One afternoon, I was strolling through cable channels and I came across a gentleman named Bill Wiese, who was giving an unforgettable description of what he saw, smelled, and heard in Hell. Mr. Wiese experienced going to Hell for twenty-three minutes. It was not a dream or near-death experience. He had published a book titled, *23 Minutes in Hell,* which is about his experience in Hell. After listening to his experience, I had the most detailed and unforgettable description of Hell and its torment. It left me feeling so much appreciation for God's love and mercy.

As Mr. Wiese described Hell, which is the absence of God, I followed along in my thoughts, imagining Hell to be extremely pitch-black. No light can be in Hell, because God is light. I later praised God for His light.

Hell is a place of pure hate and absolutely no love, because God is love. There is no love in Hell. I later praised God for all His love, joy, peace, patience, kindness, goodness, faithfulness, gentleness, and self-control.

Hell has no water or relief of burning flames, because water comes from God. I praised God for the water and food given to us.

Hell is constant violence, with screams and torments, and absolutely no peace. There is no strength, but extreme weakness in Hell, because God is the owner of everything, which includes peace, energy, and strength.

Hell has the foulest odor, described by some as far more gross than any foul odor on earth. God is the Creator of clean air, oxygen, and pleasant smells.

After imagining some of the descriptions of Hell, I felt so thankful and appreciative for God. We are so loved and wanted by God. He gives us generous gifts of love, peace, joy, water, food, clean and fresh air, rest and light, and His protection is constantly available to us. When God returns for us loving believers, He must leave behind the non-believers. All the gifts of God the non-believers are using (including love, mercy, hope, peace, food, water, wealth, and rest) go away when they enter Hell and onto the lake of fire.

Will you accept God's love into your heart? Will you accept Jesus Christ as your Lord and Savior? God's love is everlasting. Choose to love and receive love everlasting.

Part Four

UNDERSTANDING GOD'S EXTRAORDINARY FRUITS OF THE SPIRIT

THE FRUITS-OF-THE-SPIRIT BEHAVIORS WITHIN US

"But the fruit of the Spirit is love, joy, peace, patience, kindness, goodness, faithfulness, gentleness, and self-control; against such things there is no law."

GALATIANS 5:22-23 ESV

I n life, we may experience devastating or disappointing situations, causing us to feel resentment, depression, jealousy, and grief, which can cause impairment to our souls. When untreated, the heart can become hardened, making it difficult for the impaired soul to reciprocate loving behaviors. The good news is that the Holy Spirit can heal and renew our impaired minds, hearts, souls, and energy.

The Holy Spirit's supernatural power can help us experience love, joy, peace, patience, kindness, goodness, faithfulness, gentleness, and self-control. The Holy Spirit is a teacher, comforter, protector, and healer to the born-again followers of Jesus Christ. The Holy Spirit can fill you with overwhelming peace in the midst of any problems. Because of the power given to us through the Holy Spirit, we can experience the fruits of the Spirit, no matter how broken we become.

Enclosed are examples of ways to carry out your intentions for extending love, joy, peace, patience, kindness, goodness, faithfulness, gentleness, and self-control. Previously, you read how to rule over sin, which is necessary to free you from any oppression and become available to walk in the fruits of the Spirit.

Chapter Twelve

THE FRUIT OF LOVE

"But seek first the Kingdom of God and His righteousness,
and all these things shall be added to you."

MATTHEW 6:33

Have you ever pleasantly thought about someone when you go to bed and awake, and often talk to, talk about, or think of them throughout the day? How much time did you spend getting to know them before you allowed them into your heart? Did you learn a lot about them, influencing you to grow a higher level of respect and appreciation?

Will you do something for me? Will you invest the same amount of time with God?

If you currently do, outstanding! If not, read about God at least thirty minutes a day. Go to bed thinking about God. Wake up lovingly discussing God and His gifts to you with others for at least thirty minutes. Take time to pray and simply talk to God daily. You will develop respect, appreciation, and a deep love for God that is beyond measure. You will feel peace beyond measure.

Often, before we choose to open our hearts and minds to another, there are signs on whether it is a wise decision to do so. Ask yourself, "Do they produce good fruits within my life?" (The fruits of the Spirit are love, joy, peace, kindness, goodness, faithfulness, gentleness, and self-control.) Does your livelihood improve, such as good health or improved health, prosperity, your job and finances secured, shelter secured, and retirement secured?

Forming a faithful relationship with God secures your livelihood, as well as your mental and physical health. Look around you. All good things within your life come from God's generosity, including trees, plants, animals, food, minerals, rocks, water, sun, et cetera. For example, your car stems from God's generosity of His creation of rocks and other particles from the earth's crust that allow us to have metal to build cars and gasoline to drive. The flowers come from God's creation of plants. Wood, plywood, rocks, iron, metal, steel, et cetera, are used to build houses and other buildings. Look around. We are always using God's creations to build and multiply. If you let God into your heart, as much as those you deeply love, many things you righteously ask for, and believe, will be granted.

Love God immensely. Falling in love with God is one of the most rewarding experiences you will ever encounter on earth. For example, I fell in love with God in a similar way to Sue's awakening, which you will read about in this chapter. We are nothing without God. It is God's breath that is in our lungs. It is God's patience and mercy that allows me to continue to reside on earth. For I have made many mistakes, which could have rightfully shortened my time on earth.

I am so in awe of God's love for us. He loves us so much, He allowed His Son, Jesus Christ—who is too pure, too righteous, and much too clean for this dirty earth—to come down on this filthy earth that is filled with sin, evil thoughts, greed, demons, et cetera, and take mankind's place of death so that mankind can have an opportunity to live everlasting in love, purity, joy, and righteousness with God. We are so unclean that the only way we can enter into Heaven is by redemption through Jesus, who is pure. Jesus, who is perfect. Jesus, who is truly our Lord and Savior.

The two major organs required to love are the same two major organs a physician checks to deem a soul as a living human being, which is an active heart and brain. You can arrive on earth missing certain body parts and still be deemed a living human being; however, you must have an active heart and brain. Therefore, most adults have the tools to love. Some require more work than others to learn how to righteously walk in the fruits of the Spirit. Remember, love covers many sins. Righteously love.

GOD'S LOVE IS VISIBLE

Awakened by the sound of birds chirping outside of her window on a Saturday morning, Petite Sue rolled to the other side of her California king-size bed.

"All right, I will get up, so I can go running this morning," she told herself.

Sue stepped on her maplewood floors and walked to the bathroom. After showering, Sue bowed down on her knees and said, "Dear Father, lately I feel so distant from you and I want to feel your love. I feel sad and anxious for no reason. I feel so guilty about my feelings. Father, help me to feel your love again. Amen." Sue stood up, got dressed, and ate breakfast. Next, she started her daily jog from her home.

As Sue jogged, she passed a car and noticed what appeared to be bubblegum on one of the tires and a child, who was sitting in the car, holding balloons. Straight ahead, she saw kids playing basketball. Moving right along, Sue took notice of a bee moving from plant to plant. Her neighbor was about to water the plants and dust off his rocks. She greeted her neighbor, as she passed by. He smiled and nodded his head, as a "hello" gesture. This was a normal routine. But what happened next was not. Sue began to think about a TV show she watched yesterday, saying how metal comes from the crust of God's earth, and the earth's crust was made of different types of rocks.

"Wait!" Sue said to herself, as she stopped jogging. Sue suddenly had an epiphany. Her thoughts rewound to her neighbor's rocks. Sue then visualized turning her doorknob, which was made from metal. She began to think, *What else am I using that comes directly from God?* She visualized opening her door, which was made from wood, which came from God's trees, and walking onto her living room carpet, which was made from wool and other fibers and textures, which came from the hair of God's sheep and other animals. She now visualized sitting at her dining room table, covered with a silk tablecloth, whose silk came from God's silkworms. Sue saw herself eating oatmeal and strawberries, and sipping tea from a glass cup. Tea comes from God's plants. The glass she drank from was made from God's fire and sand. Afterwards, Sue arose, walked into the kitchen and onto her tile floors, which came from God's clay and sand. Sue went to the refrigerator. She got two servings of leftover banana pudding. Her bananas were another one of God's creations for us.

Suddenly, she snapped out of her epiphany and started jogging again, and with more speed, because she thought about those added calories from the banana pudding. While jogging, Sue thought some more about her epiphany, which was her visibly seeing God's generosity and love surrounding her. Sue started to cry when she became aware that

God's love and generosity was all around her. She now felt His love and closeness again. As she jogged, Sue continued seeking God in all that she viewed. She returned home feeling so loved.

Look around. What are you using that comes from God's creations, such as the earth's crust, plants, trees, sun, sand, fire, rocks, and animals? Sue's story is an example of having her prayers answered, and God giving her ways to maintain an intimate relationship with Him. Read on to identify additional ways to keep your heart and mind on God.

APPRECIATING GOD'S VISIBLE LOVE

How often do you spend time appreciating God's visible love? God's trees and plants entrap dust and airborne particles, which help prevent damage to our lungs. The trees also help absorb the harmful carbon dioxide and release oxygen. Sue's running shoes, the little girl's balloon, the basketball, and the tires on the car are all made from rubber, and rubber comes from God's *Hevea brasiliens* (natural rubber) trees. Bed sheets, pillowcases, curtains, clothes, et cetera, are made from God's generosity of plants, such as linen and cotton. Experts say that the decomposition of God's dead plants and animals from an exceptionally long time ago are some of the resources used today to make gasoline for our vehicles, electricity, and different forms of metal. The crust of God's earth is used for almost every valuable thing; a major one is metal. There are different types of metal, such as steel, iron, aluminum, et cetera, which can be used for many things, such as Sue's doorknobs, house, cars, and buildings. God's sun generously provides Vitamin D, which contributes to strong bones. Vitamin D also helps our bodies in other ways. For starters, Sue would not be able to take a long jog without strong bones.

Humans have also become aware of how to use the extraordinary energy from the sun to help provide some of the electricity for houses, factories, power lines, and many other things that rely heavily on electricity. The sun is one of God's beautiful stars. God's generosity of stars helps us in many ways. Stars can be used as the measurement of time and give light (refer to Matthew 2:2 and Genesis 1:14-19). Stars can be used as a location guide. Stars have contributed to producing light, heat, ultraviolet rays, x-rays, and other forms of radiation, which we use in significant ways. The moon helps make it possible for us to experience twenty-four hours in a day, because the moon helps extend the measurement of time within a day.

Wind helps us with pollination by blowing pollen grains, which cause the male antler of the plant to blow and stick to the female stigma of a plant, contributing to more production of seeds. Humans, animals, and plants also depend greatly on pollination. Pollination consists of insects, such as butterflies and bees, going from plant to plant, and in doing so, the male antler of the plant may stick to the female stigma of the plant, producing more seeds. So, the next time you see an insect, feel appreciative of the things they do for us. The insect and wind pollination help produce more and more seeds, which grow to become fruits and vegetables. Of the hundreds of different types of fruits and vegetables, how many of those do you eat? Show more appreciation to God by adding more fruits, vegetables, and nuts to your meals.

Clouds are made of waterdrops or ice crystals. When the clouds build up, this results in greater drops that fall to the earth; the familiar term for this is called rainwater. Clouds of different shapes and sizes help predict the weather. Clouds can help us move to safety from a potential storm.

Every day, become aware of at least one of God's creations that you see, hear, taste, smell, or feel, and how it expresses love to you. For example, say you view a bee when you look outside your window. The bee provides pollination, which multiplies more and more produce to eat, purchase, sell, or give to others. The bees also provide honey that tastes delicious. Experts say honey can help prevent certain diseases, increase athletic performance, prevent coughing, et cetera. Wow, God gives us so many gifts to be thankful and express gratitude for.

JESUS' LOVE HEALED ME

A middle-aged mother named Lashaun told me that Jesus healed her from breast cancer. Lashaun had recently left an abusive relationship when she became aware of the growing cancer cells within her breast. She was staying at a shelter for women, who were victims of domestic violence.

Not only did she have breast cancer, but it was at a high stage. Lashaun was in so much pain at the time, she could not do her chores at the shelter. As a result, she was evicted from the shelter. Lashaun was faced with being homeless, leaving her kids without a mom, and possibly dying.

Lashaun knew who could turn her life around. His name is Jesus.

Lashaun moved in with her mom. She poured out her heart and soul to Jesus. Lashaun submitted her life over to Jesus.

Soon after, she returned to the cancer treatment center. Before the staff began treatment, she asked to hold hands and pray. The majority of the staff prayed with her. Those who did not, she prayed for them. Her test results were astonishing to the physician. There was no detectable cancer to treat. From that day forward, Lashaun witnessed to whomever she spoke to that Jesus is her Lord and Savior, and Jesus healed her. Her new focus was to be a witness for Jesus Christ and to restore her life.

My brief encounter with Lashaun was years after she was healed from breast cancer. Her appreciation for Jesus' healing was so strong. It was as if Jesus had just healed her that day. As she witnessed to me, her love and appreciation for Jesus was so evident. Lashaun's life had done a 360-degree turn for the better. She married a man who loves Jesus, she enrolled in school to attain her master's degree, her kids were doing well, she financially supported her mom, and she had just built a beautiful home.

It has now been years since I had the pleasure of talking to Lashaun. If I could meet her again, I would ask so many questions. Her love and commitment to witness for Jesus was so strong and loving. I would love to see the energy that flows from her loving heart and mind whenever she talks about Jesus.

SELF-LOVE

As we extend loving behaviors to others, let us complete a checklist to ensure we are providing an adequate amount of self-love. God has generously provided us with tools to express love to our bodies, minds, souls, and spirits. Claim your title as a reborn Christian. Claim your power you receive through the Holy Spirit in Jesus Christ's name. Speak good health, protection, wealth, and joy over your body, mind, soul, and spirit.

Say the following prayer:

In the name of Jesus Christ with the power of the Holy Spirit, I claim that every cell, tissue, organ, muscle, nerve, and all blood within my body is in perfect health. Through Jesus Christ, I wear the armor of salvation and carry the word of God with great courage. In Jesus' name, I command all unclean spirits and forces to stay more than 10,000 feet away from by my body, mind, soul, and spirit. I give thanks to everyone in God's Kingdom and all the Holy Angels who have been granted by God to surround and protect my body, mind, soul, and spirit. Amen.

Believe and memorize all of God's promises. Recite some daily. Pray for God to reveal your role in the body of Christ as a born-again Christian. Aim to work hard for God.

"And whatever you do, do it heartily, as to the Lord and not to men."
COLOSSIANS 3:23

God provides each of us with spiritual gifts and assignments. Below are some examples for you to try and discern which ones closely match to you:

- Intercessory prayer for others' healing and blessings.

- Renounce demons.

- Pray for God to provide prophetic dreams to instruct you toward your spiritual talent.

- Teach the gospel.

- Win souls to Christ through ministering, singing, acting, or writing Christian-based materials.

- At times, serve others (such as giving a trusted neighbor who is having car problems a ride to work).

- Arrange a prayer line in your family or Christian group.

- If you love to sing, join a Christian choir.

- Write down your dreams and ask God to provide you with the gift of interpreting dreams to provide edification to Christians.

Once you identify your spiritual gifts, set aside time to learn and develop your God-given gifts. Strive to implement your abilities in the body of Christ and offer your services to as many people as you can. Identifying your role in the body of Christ can provide a sense of feeling secure and grounded, because God will always keep you employed and provide all that you need to flourish your talent. Knowing your position with God allows you to feel secure.

LOVE OTHERS

God the Father, the Son, the Holy Spirit, and Holy Angels, and your loved ones would be the best choices to begin to love. As your heart grows, continue to guard it wisely, while slowly opening your heart to love more people.

A great way to become more aware and appreciative of the love you are receiving, whether it's from your pet, parents, child, friend, neighbor, relative, or church member, et cetera, is to recollect their acts of expressing love to you. Simply calling to say, "How are you doing?" giving a hug, attending a meaningful event, et cetera, can be acts motivated out of love for you.

LOVING BEHAVIORS TOWARD OTHERS

In the Bible, Paul taught the Christians that Jesus encourages us to serve one another. God has blessed us with opportunities to serve others.

Many services do not require you to spend money. Discover your family's and friends' goals. Commit to praying for them to achieve their goals. A feeling of appreciation may be experienced within you and the recipient. Extend generosity by allowing another citizen to go ahead of you in such spaces as a parking space, store aisle, or a driving lane. Leave a few minutes earlier to encourage patience with others at stores, events, parking lots, and with motorists on the road. Visualize everyone in the world being kind, patient, and generous to one another.

Remember that our five communicators have energy and assist with manifesting our thoughts, words, images, beliefs, and efforts within the environment. This step is a great contribution to manifesting peace within the atmosphere. Use kind words in your daily encounters with people and animals. Accept an invite to someone's birthday, graduation, seminar, et cetera, or provide a card, gift, or verbal acknowledgement of their special day. Rejoice with them. Forgive others for their mistakes and imperfections. Communicate how much you love and appreciate the loving behaviors that God's creations are contributing to the earth by using your thoughts, words, emotions, images, and actions. An example of the words you can say is "I love you," to the sun, moon, trees, animals, and people. An action you apply can be recycling, which can help God's earth. Start and end each day expressing love to God the Father, the Son, and the Holy Spirit, along with the Holy Angels, the self, and others.

Chapter Thirteen

THE FRUIT OF FORGIVENESS

While Jesus was being murdered on the cross, his loving heart asked God to forgive us. Jesus said in Luke 23:34, "Father, forgive them, for they do not know what they do." Jesus' heart was of great compassion, while he was being tormented and slowly dying because of our sins. This impacts me to feel a sense of duty to forgive all whom I believe have hurt me. Forgiveness is one of the greatest gifts to give oneself.

Forgive yourself for the mistakes you have made, which may have caused pain. Unforgiveness, resentment, guilt, and anger are very toxic. These are harmful to your body, releasing toxins on your organs.

Everyone will experience hurt because we have a sinful nature, and part of our journey is forgiving, learning from our mistakes, and moving toward love. Pursue loving good and righteous things, which make you happy.

In regard to forgiving others, remember that God has forgiven you, me, and others for our sins, so pay it forward and forgive everyone who has hurt you. Unforgiveness also invites demons to come and taunt you, sending thoughts to heighten your feelings of blame, hate, anger, envy, or possibly the want to hurt the accused. Unforgiveness can be a hinderance to Heaven.

Think about how much God has forgiven us, despite our mistakes and sins. God has accepted our repentance of sin. He gave His Son as a sacrificial offering, so we can be given everlasting life. God's Son was killed. His Son, who is loving and perfect. God forgives us. We have an obligation to forgive others and spread love throughout the world. However, do not stay in abusive relationships or toxic environments. Seek professional guidance for advice on these types of relationships. Sometimes it's necessary to forgive and leave the relationship.

"Judge not, and you shall not be judged. Condemn not, and you shall not be condemned. Forgive, and you will be forgiven."

LUKE 6:37

Daily admission of sin with the intent of not repeating that sin is a huge step in the right direction. After you genuinely repent, ask God to forgive you of all your sins and your family members' sins. When we repent, turn away from sin, and ask for forgiveness of possible generational sin, such as lust, theft, gossip, witchcraft, idolatry, gluttony, poverty, unforgiveness, et cetera, we may free ourselves and future generations from that generational curse.

FORGIVE LIKE JESUS FORGIVES

Reflect on the fact that our Savior, Jesus, experienced a slow, agonizing pain and death on the cross so that we can have an inheritance of curses removed, healing from illnesses, and everlasting life. Jesus, who is sinless, made the sacrificial offering for our sins by being crucified on the cross. Jesus stayed faithful, loving Judas even though He knew Judas would betray Him.

Who is Judas?

"Then one of the twelve, called Judas Iscariot, went to the chief priests and said, 'What are you willing to give me if I deliver Him to you?' And they counted out to him thirty pieces of silver. So from that time he sought opportunity to betray Him."

MATHEW 26:14-16

"When evening had come, He sat down with the twelve. Now as they were eating, He said, 'Assuredly I say to you, one of you will betray Me.' And they were exceedingly sorrowful, and each of them began to say to Him, 'Lord, is it I?' He answered and said, 'He who dipped his hand with Me in the dish will betray Me. The Son of Man indeed goes just as it is written of Him, but woe to that man by whom the Son of Man is betrayed! It would have been good for that man if he had not been born.' Then Judas, who was betraying Him, answered and said, 'Rabbi, is it I?' He said to him, 'You have said it.'"

MATTHEW 26:20-25

"And while He was still speaking, behold, a multitude; and he who was called Judas, one of the twelve, went before them and drew near to Jesus to kiss him. But Jesus said to him, 'Judas, are you betraying the Son of Man with a kiss?'"

LUKE 22:47-48

Although Jesus was given this prophecy before it came to pass, He continued to love Judas and others. Such an act of unconditional love and forgiveness from Jesus should inspire believers to let go of unforgiveness. Repent and forgive others daily. Forgiveness frees us to maintain a loving state of mind.

"I've never liked you!" Geraldine yelled at her sister Martha, during an argument they had while playing a game. Things spiraled downward after Martha heard those hurtful words. Geraldine did not apologize. Buried in Martha's broken heart was pain, because her big sister she always admired said such unloving and hurtful words.

Martha had always wondered why her big sister would criticize her about everything. Geraldine never wanted Martha to hang out with her and her friends. Now, Martha believed she had the answer. They never spoke about the argument. In the past, Martha would beg her sister to let her tag along, but now she began to focus on friends instead of her sister Geraldine. When they became adults, they were cordial at their family gatherings, but Martha relinquished her desire to have a close relationship with her sister a long time ago and Geraldine never pursued her.

Years later, Martha became a disciple for Jesus Christ, and over time, she forgave Geraldine and asked God to heal Geraldine's stony heart toward her.

Geraldine and Martha now communicate almost weekly. Martha says learning how much Jesus has done for us, despite how humans betrayed and attacked Him, helped to open her heart to forgive her sister. This is an example of forgiving as God expects us to forgive. Martha learned about Jesus' love and overwhelming forgiveness and applied that teaching within her own life. What have you learned about forgiveness and applied within your life?

ESTABLISH HEALTHY RELATIONSHIPS ONLY

(Toxic relationships can hurt you in multiple ways, including financially.)

Opening our hearts to extend love is one of the greatest experiences on earth. But in doing so, we may also sometimes experience a broken heart. This is why it is very important to forgive, which will contribute to us being able to extend love continuously to others. Martha and Geraldine's story is an example of experiencing a broken heart and unforgiveness being transformed into forgiveness and extending love again. Forgiveness does not mean you must stay in a toxic relationship, but rather you let go of the offense. This allows our hearts to continue to love, which may or may not include the ones who hurt us. However, take steps to ensure that the offense is not repeated by the individuals. We must also protect our hearts to discern to whom we are equally yoked to give our hearts. That includes choosing a spouse and our friends. We are not a match for everyone, so we must choose wisely to whom we give our hearts. Healthy relationships have less toxicity to forgive than unhealthy relationships.

"Above all else, guard your heart, for everything you do flows from it."

PROVERBS 4:23 NIV

Ask yourself, when deciding to whom to extend your heart, does the relationship inspire you to walk in the fruits of the Spirit? Or does the relationship influence you to allow more demons into your life? Choose carefully to whom you give your thoughts, words, emotions, images, and time. Pray to God and seek the Holy Spirit's and Holy Angels' guidance to decipher who would be an equally yoked friend, spouse, and employer. They should be a revolving door of fruits-of-the-Spirit behaviors. Pray for peace, love, and tranquility within all of your encounters. Please pray, fast, and be patient for an answer, before you make a life-altering decision, such as to date, marry, get a roommate, adopt a pet, change careers, sign an agreement, adopt a child, divorce, travel, et cetera. Pray, fast, and patiently wait to receive instructions and guidance from the Holy Spirit.

Sometimes, I know what the Holy Spirit advises me to do regarding my upcoming choices. Like everyone else, I have the free will to choose what has been advised or go my own path. My consultation from the Holy Spirit comes through visons, dreams, sounds, strong intuition, discernment of spirits, and sometimes by revisiting Bible-based stories with similar dilemmas.

Remember: pray, consult, fast, and be patient for revelation.

Stay far away from encounters that conjure inappropriate emotions (such as jealousy, rage, lust, et cetera) and thoughts, which can lead to sin. Ask for assistance from the Holy Spirit to rebuke any demons, which may be involved in instigating your inappropriate feelings and thoughts.

Refrain from instantly responding to someone who has been unfair or disrespectful. Resist the temptation to retaliate. Ask for assistance from the Holy Spirit to rebuke any demons that may be involved.

HONESTY

Forgiveness includes being honest. When you experience an offense by someone, review your actions. Was there anything you could have previously done to prevent the offense? For example, were there red flags along the way? Did you leave when you initially saw the red flags? Did you address them? Remember that forgiveness does not mean giving a pass to red flags and getting more involved with the offender. If you experience red flags, such as being hurt in the beginning of the relationship, forgive the offender. Consult God on whether you should move forward with a relationship with them. If you are experiencing red flags, or any type of pain, during the start of the relationship, 99.9 percent of the time you should not get more involved with them.

Do you consult, pray, and wait for a response from God before you make decisions? Remember, Daniel waited twenty-one days. God's response may not always come immediately, or through dreams, visions, and prophets. Sometimes, to receive your answer, you are required to go slow to form a new relationship. This can prevent getting close to toxic and harmful people. While taking your time, ask God to gift you with the ability to discern the spirits within a person. If you did not take precautions and go slow, as scripture advises us to do, be honest with yourself. Take accountability for your errors and forgive yourself. This will help free you to forgive the offender for their actions.

EXERCISE THE PHYSICAL BODY AND EAT HEALTHY

Our physical and mental health endures a lot when we experience hurt and unforgiveness, especially if it is a devastation to us. For example, a young lady named Tam ate poorly and neglected her health for years. She had multiple cavities with no pain for years. Then, one day, she experienced being hurt by her ex-boyfriend. Days after the offense, Tam was still seething in anger and unforgiveness. She woke up with a large hole in one of her cavities, a throbbing toothache in another tooth, and an earache, and she overall felt ill for a week. Harmful toxins can be released within the body from prolonged anger, rage, jealousy, grief, unforgiveness, et cetera. An unhealthy body like Tam's may experience a more negative impact than a healthy body. Forgiveness positively impacts the body, sending some of the harmful toxins away. Practice a good health routine, and the physical body will more likely remain strong, even during our rough times.

I was having a business conversation on the telephone with a gentleman named Dave, when I heard an energetic voice in the background. Dave kindly apologized for interrupting our conversation to reply to the soft, energetic voice I heard in the background. He went on to say it was his ninety-one-year-old mother and she was telling him she was ready to go riding.

I was surprised by her age, because she sounded more likely to be around sixty years old. I complimented her zest and inquired about what strategies she applied in life to have so much energy.

He went on to share that his mother took good care of her family and herself throughout her life. Every morning, while oatmeal was slowly cooking on the stove, she exercised. She did not cook fried food, never ate fast food, had no sugar added to her food, and she used only herbs for seasoning. Every day she ensured her kids were physically active, even if it was simply walking. He went on to say she was in the best health to be expected for her age. She had no cancers or illnesses. He proudly told me, at his old age, he never had any cavities.

Their story is an inspiration to take care of our bodies. I'm quite sure they went through their period of pain and unforgiveness. However, their bodies (Wow! Never had cavities!) stand in good health from healthy habits.

Chapter Fourteen

THE FRUIT OF JOY

"Whom [Jesus Christ] having not seen you love. Though now you do not see
Him, yet believing, you rejoice with joy inexpressible and full of glory."

1 PETER 1:8

H OW OFTEN DO YOU FEEL JOY?
As I was driving to one of my seminars titled "Showing Yourself
and Others Unconditional Love," I was feeling excited that I was fulfilling
one of my purposes in life. Overwhelming joy flourished from the crown
of my head to the soles of my feet. It was a feeling greater than the
purchase of a home or the publishing of a book.

I believe it was my comforter, the Holy Spirit, who generously released
joy throughout my body. The Holy Spirit will help us in our efforts to live
a joyful life. Leading people to Christ, through the path of love, is a sure
way to experience joy from the Holy Spirit.

That entire week, prior to my first seminar, my thoughts, words,
emotions, images, actions, taste, touch, hearing, sight, and smell mainly
centered around God's unconditional love. I looked for God's love in the

food, trees, or anything else I put my sight on, listened to, ate, et cetera, much like Sue, whom I discussed in "God's Love is Visible."

Although the Holy Spirit has the power to do insurmountable things for us to experience joy, the Holy Spirit will respect our free will in choosing our own experiences, which comes from a compilation of our thoughts, words, emotions, images, actions, taste, touch, hearing, sight, and smell. I believe my choice to seek God with my heart, soul, mind, and strength at that time welcomed the Holy Spirit to reciprocate overwhelming love and joy toward me.

To seek God is to seek love. To experience God's love is an overflowing feeling of joy throughout the body. God is so loving; in addition to sending the Holy Spirit to comfort us with bliss, God also gifted humans with "feel-good" neurotransmitters that humans are empowered to turn on. This empowers us to navigate our experiences of happiness.

However, just like everything else, you must apply faith and work. Would you be willing to develop the heart and mind to such a level of pure happiness? Think about how much time and effort it took you to do such things as build good credit, purchase a home, graduate, build a close relationship with your loved one, et cetera. I would imagine it required time and effort. The same goes for building a close and loving relationship with God. It requires your time and effort.

Get started by applying your thoughts, words, emotions, images, and actions to all of the things God has done for you. The highest level of joy we can experience is to deeply love God. Use your spiritual gifts to win souls to believe Jesus Christ is our Lord and Savior. As you reciprocate love to God, your entire essence encounters a glorious experience. You experience the "feel-good" chemicals God gifted our bodies to possess, such as dopamine, endorphins, oxytocin, serotonin, along with other "feel-good" chemicals within us. Most days we can release those happy chemicals God has within us. As you build a life walking in the fruits of the Spirit, you begin to experience those "feel-good" chemicals frequently.

Below are more ways to experience those "feel-good" chemicals, such as dopamine, endorphins, oxytocin, serotonin, along with other "feel-good" chemicals God has created within us, which help us to continuously feel God's joy.

DOING THINGS THAT CAN HELP BRING JOY TO THE BODY

- Working toward your goals can turn on dopamine. For example, you can write down your goals, as seeing the progress of reaching your goal can turn on dopamine. You can create and accomplish a small, daily challenge, which can turn on dopamine. For example, I do a sixteen-hour fast from 7:00 p.m. to 11:00 a.m. and reward myself with a nice meal.

- Feeling relied upon in a positive way can turn on serotonin. For example, you can facilitate a Bible study or prayer group.

- Volunteer to help others learn that Jesus is our Lord and Savior.

- Trusting others brings about oxytocin. For example, you can trust God. Trust Jesus. Trust the Holy Spirit. Trust the Holy Angels.

- Laughter stimulates endorphins. Decide to laugh every day. For example, purchase a comedy book, watch a comedy show, play with kids or animals, or play games and sports for fun, which can all turn on endorphins.

- Exercise can possibly turn on endorphins.

- Listen to music that uplifts you, which can turn on dopamine. Ensure it's positive music.

- Start your day in the right direction by getting enough sleep, which can help turn on dopamine.

DOING THINGS THAT CAN HELP BRING JOY TO THE MIND

- Commit to a role in the body of Christ you believe positively impacts others. For example, designate a time to pray every day for the self and others, volunteer to bring a child to church every Sunday, free an animal from the shelter, et cetera. With faith, say edifying affirmations twenty or more times when you first awake. An example of an affirmation: "I will have a beautiful and blessed day. In Jesus' name, amen." This can turn on serotonin.

- Commit to adjusting your attitude to be renewed daily.

- Create daily goals. Reward yourself daily for accomplishing your daily goals. For example, if every day, you exercise for thirty minutes and drink enough water, the reward may be to watch one positive movie that day. This can turn on dopamine.

- Bond regularly. Verbally express to your loved ones that you love them. Give a hug or a smile. Spend time with family, friends, and pets. This can turn on oxytocin.

- Maintain a clean environment. Clutter can cause one to feel stressed. Cleaning requires us to bend, lift, squat, and simply move around, which is excellent exercise for the body. Clean your bathroom on Monday, kitchen on Tuesday, car on Wednesday, et cetera, or wake up early to clean your home, or clean up right after you use something. Design a schedule that accommodates your lifestyle. This can diffuse stress.

- Praise God daily for everything, while feeling that more blessings are being added. For example, go throughout the day feeling excited that a check is in the mail, large enough to attain the things you desire. This may release dopamine, oxytocin, endorphins, and serotonin.

- If you feel your mood is going down or wake up feeling down, immediately renounce the spirit of oppression. For example, read a deliverance prayer and say, "In the name of Jesus with the power of the Holy Spirit, I renounce you, spirit of oppression! Get out and do not return." Say it until you feel your strength restoring itself.

- Communicate to God seven things you are thankful for receiving. For example, you might say, "Thank you, God, for my relationship with You, my perfect health, my career, taking care of my family, my friends, my pets, the beautiful tile, which comes from Your gift of clay, et cetera." As you name the things you are sincerely thankful for in your life, you may start to feel appreciative, which may turn on dopamine, oxytocin, endorphins, and serotonin.

Chapter Fifteen

THE FRUIT OF PEACE

"You will keep him *in perfect peace,* whose *mind* is *stayed* on *You,*

because he trusts in You."

ISAIAH 26:3

A devoted Christian named Tarsha reached for her garage fob, then gasped with fear, because she realized it and her wallet were at the boutique. Inside the wallet were several hundred dollars and credit cards.

While she was speeding to the boutique, an unexplainable peace came upon her. It felt almost like a very relaxed sedation. As a result, her breathing calmed down and she began to slow down and drive the speed limit. She turned on the radio. While pleading to God for her wallet to be recovered, the lyrics of the song on the radio were saying, "Jesus is going to work it out." She arrived at the boutique. She felt reassured, both from the overwhelming peace that came upon her and the message through the song, everything was going to be okay. She was correct. Someone turned in her wallet and everything was intact.

When she returned to her car, she joyfully thanked and praised the Lord.

Although her fight or flight system immediately activated, and her body's response was to feel high doses of stress when she realized she left her wallet, the Holy Spirit doused her with an overwhelming peace and reminded her she is never alone. When a devoted Christian falls, God allows the Holy Spirit and Holy Angels to be available for their rescue.

"And we know that all things work together for good to those who love God, to those who are the called according to His purpose."

ROMANS 8:28

PEACE IN THE MIDST OF CHALLENGES

Tom woke up to the smell of breakfast. He went into the kitchen, and his son said, "Good morning, Pops. I am cooking us some omelets and hash browns. Breakfast will be ready in a few minutes."

Tom replied, "Thank you, son."

Tom got dressed and sat at the table. He said grace and ate his breakfast. They chuckled back and forth about sports and what was going on in their lives. Tom washed the dishes after eating the breakfast that his son cooked, and his son did the same when Tom cooked.

The harmony between Tom and his son is pretty much how Tom's day goes when he is driving to work, while he is at work, shopping at the store, playing golf after work, and when he returns home. His encounters are peaceful.

What about when your kids, pets, roommates, or loved ones are being defiant? It can interrupt a peaceful breakfast, day at work, or fun activity. It is more challenging to feel at peace when we are not in harmony with those we adore, or multiple disappointments are occurring. Incorporate these actions into your life for greater peace:

- Pray to the Holy Spirit and ask for guidance on obtaining peace and healing within your relationships.

- Ask the Holy Angels for assistance.

- Visualize smiling and receiving love, prosperity, perfect health, and assistance.

- Begin to thank God, Jesus, the Holy Spirit, and Holy Angels for restoring you and providing peace within you.

- Feel hopeful that a beautiful change is taking place, because disappointments are temporary. The fact that we have God's gifts and blessings to manifest peace is joyful! To maintain peace, keep your mind on scriptures, such as Proverbs 1:33, which says, "But whoever listens to me will dwell safely, and will be secure, without fear of evil."

As we actively listen and seek God's instructions, we elevate our results in life to be fair, peaceful, and loving. Because God is a just and loving Father, He will always give you the most loving, fair, and peaceful solution.

Proceed to apply love, joy, peace, patience, kindness, goodness, faithfulness, gentleness, and self-control throughout your day as God instructs us to do.

WAYS TO LIVE A LIFE OF PEACE

- Provide peaceful encounters to people, animals, plants, and the earth. When we are good to others, good and peaceful encounters come to us.

- Make appointments that include extra time for possible, unforeseen setbacks, such as if your doctor's office is late seeing patients or the cashier is waiting on assistance to get an override. Such thoughtfulness allows less stress to surface within your encounters, making it easier to be kind during unforeseen setbacks. How would family, friends, merchants, and coworkers rate their interactions with you? Is it peaceful, kind, gentle, calm, and uplifting, or is it annoying, controlling, overbearing, manipulative, and combative? Memorize daily one of God's scriptures regarding peace. Calamity will keep its distance from you if you do not lie, steal, hurt, judge, or manipulate others. Create sacred places to commune with God. Surround yourself while in your environment with peaceful items, such as the cross and inspiring words. Remove decorations that worship other gods or inspire non-righteous behaviors.

- Fulfill your obligations to your employer, creditors, household, and others that you agreed upon.

Remember, pain is for a season and it will pass. Only love can last forever. The Bible provides plenty of stories where people went through seasons of pain; however, they were redeemed with blessings. For example:

1. Sarah went through a season of being barren before she was blessed with her own son.

2. Esau went through a season of being enraged over the loss of his inheritance to his brother before he established lots of land, family, and stocks.

3. Joseph went through a season of slavery before he became one of the most powerful men in Egypt.

Chapter Sixteen

THE FRUIT OF PATIENCE

"Be completely humble and gentle; be patient, bearing with one another in love."

EPHESIANS 4:2 NIV

P atience is the ability to endure extended discomfort with kindness. Allot yourself and others some extra time for unplanned experiences you may come upon. Patience is a behavior that God asks of us. Remember, Daniel fasted and prayed for twenty-one days before he received an answer to his prayer. Patience is worth investing time and energy. As you build a day-to-day, intimate relationship with God, you will become more aware of the multiple duties assigned to you in the Kingdom of God. To do so requires patience and consistency.

Encounters with strangers are perfect opportunities to exercise patience. When you go to the store or drive on the highway, allot enough time for the lady stalling to close her car door, which is delaying you to drive into the parking space, or the guy choosing to drive his bicycle in the middle of the road and the goose walking slowly across the street.

Here's another example: One morning, while driving, you see instructions to take a detour because of a marathon ahead. This is a perfect opportunity to utilize your five communicators to extend patience. Apply the following thoughts: *All is well. I allotted extra time today.* Apply these words: "Holy Spirit and Holy Angels, provide safety to the participants in the marathon." Apply these emotions: Feel patient and empowered for maintaining a high-level energy due to patience, instead of lowering your energy because of feeling angry and impatient from running late, et cetera.

In the beginning, take small steps, day by day, and increase your efforts as time progresses. You will build a momentum of love energy that feels so rewarding. Yes, some days may be discouraging, as we do have bad days, but overall, you would not prefer life to be any other way.

Have you ever experienced feeling impatient to the point where you felt angry and decided to move out of one grocery line to another, or drive from one lane to another, only to experience going slower? Do not be impatient. Energy from being impatient is problematic. It draws more impatient people and problematic circumstances to you. Love energy moves faster and without interruption, but with clarity, perfection, and peace. You will draw more peace into your life when you are patient.

CHOOSE PATIENCE OVER IMPATIENCE

One morning, a floor installer came and installed wood for Beatrice's floors. The floors looked immaculate.

Oops.

The next day when Beatrice went into her living room, she drew back her blinds and saw a small section of the floor that the installer apparently forgot to complete. Immediately, she called him. No answer. She left a voicemail using a friendly and gentle tone. She prayed that the issue would be resolved peacefully. She chose to think positively, by telling herself that he was probably doing another job and had put away his phone.

The installer returned her call later that day and acknowledged that he forgot to go back and complete that portion. Beatrice accepted his apology and waited for him to return the next day. He returned and finished the job. Beatrice exercised patience and they ended on a good note.

You're probably thinking that's how Beatrice and the installer should have interacted. Well, I have seen the simplest errors snowball, because of a non-loving (opposite of fruits-of-the-Spirit behaviors) approach. I have seen situations where a person is so impatient and builds up so much frustration or fear, they lose phone signal, or other mishaps happen, such as the customer loses the installer's telephone number. Then, the customer contacts the company's customer service representative, who forgets to submit a request for the technician to go back and finish the job, or the request to go back was added on the wrong account.

Yes, things are most likely to go to shambles when we are impatient. Patience includes God's love energy, so it moves with clarity, calmness, perfection, and peace, and is more productive than impatient energy. The energy from hurrying out of impatience or fear moves slower. It is problematic and less productive, because of the accidents, fear, errors, confusion, conflict, et cetera, that are manifested when we are impatient.

TIPS ON IMPROVING PATIENCE

Start your day by allowing yourself and others extra time for any unforeseen delay, such as misplacing keys, et cetera. It is easier to be kind and patient when you are not feeling anxiety from being pressed for more time.

Pray for the self and others to walk in the spirit of patience. Memorize Philippians 4:6: "Be anxious for nothing, but in everything by prayer and supplication, with thanksgiving, let your requests be made known to God."

Remember, patience is a fruit-of-the-Spirit behavior, which means love energy is involved. When you choose to be patient, you choose to maintain a high energy level, instead of problematic energy from being impatient. It may appear that one is moving faster when he or she impatiently hurries through a situation; however, a higher risk of making mistakes comes with impatience. Have you hurried to do something and made an error from feeling pressured, and then had to go back and start over again? Patience prevents unnecessary errors.

If you are going through struggling times, such as car problems, tension between you and others, buying or selling your home, et cetera, stay aware that exercising patience allows your resolution to come faster and without interruption. Each day you are getting closer and closer to a resolution. Create images of the issue being resolved. Change your emotion to a feeling of belief and faith. Act and feel as if everything is resolved and well. Pray for wisdom on how to resolve the issue effectively and expedite its resolution. It will soon pass, just as all problems pass. Pray in the name of Jesus and with the power of the Holy Spirit that any demons involved in these barriers are to be rebuked.

If you feel frustrated with someone, then pray and ask God to help you extend more patience. Apply the following: Take time to understand their perspective before you provide your feedback to them; remain gentle and soft with your words; ask questions and do not accuse.

Chapter Seventeen

THE FRUIT OF KINDNESS

"Therefore, whatever you want men to do to you,
do also to them, for this is the Law and the Prophets."

MATTHEW 7:12

A kind person often extends care to others, puts forth effort to prevent others' inconveniences, and applies effort to accommodate. How often do you evaluate how your choices impact others? When you must make changes in your life, such as to stop carpooling, give prior notice, so those who will be impacted can make other arrangements. Whenever we make changes and others are involved, we should evaluate how others may be impacted. Consider ways to make your changes while maintaining peace toward others. Sometimes, advance notice is all that is needed, which will allow others time to adjust.

God is the greatest expression of kindness. God gifts us with His Son, Jesus Christ. God's provision of a variety of foods alone is an extraordinary expression of kindness. God's many resources available to help our bodies, minds, souls, and spirits is extremely kind. Just as God does so many things for us daily, we should leap at the opportunity to spread kindness. For example, kindness might be letting someone with one or two items of groceries go ahead of you in the grocery line, returning carts to the inside of the store that someone had left on the road, choosing not to litter, and picking up store items that were left on the floor in the store.

What other acts of kindness can we do daily? Simply smiling, greeting people, and communicating with a gentle tone can be a huge act of kindness to others. What about challenging personalities, such as pessimistic and confrontational personalities? Teach them how to treat you by what you allow and do not allow. If someone acts unpleasant and says unkind words about you and this is a one-time encounter, such as a stranger in the grocery store, pray, forgive, and move on quietly. If this is someone you will reencounter, pray, forgive, and share with them how unpleasant the hurtful words caused you to feel. Share with them how you would prefer them to interact with you and allow them the opportunity to change their behavior. If they express remorse, accept their apology. If they intentionally continue to say hurtful things and this is a valued relationship, obtain unbiased mediators (such as a therapist, pastor, or other trusted confidant) to help resolve with love. If this is an acquaintance, coworker, or a casual friend, create distance from the very beginning of their offense.

Also, review your thoughts, words, emotions, images, and actions, and make sure you are not igniting contention and causing anyone to feel unpleasant feelings, unnecessary inconvenience, or harm. Are your words kind? Do you speak with a gentle and respectful tone? This includes children, animals, and the elderly. We are not perfect, and therefore at times, our impact on others may be negative. Edifying feedback is beneficial, but mean words are not.

KIND INTERACTIONS CAN BRING UPON AN UPLIFTED SPIRIT

Below are some examples of kind interactions.

A homeless gentleman asked twenty-six-year-old Daija for some change as she walked into the gas station. She apologized and told him she only had a debit card. While in the gas station, she used the ATM inside. Daija believes the Holy Spirit came upon her to get twenty dollars in cash from her debit card and give it to the homeless gentleman. Daija adhered to her thought. She stepped out of the gas station and kindly gave the gentleman above his request.

Joni strived to be a servant for God. When twenty-year-old Joni cashed her paycheck, she purchased ripe fruits and vegetables, which she distributed to those at the homeless shelter. The shelters near Joni provided mostly high-sodium, sugary, and fatty foods. Joni purchased oranges, apples, strawberries, walnuts, pistachios, cashews, carrots, et cetera, as a way of helping others receive nutrients to their bodies. Joni's act made her feel she was fulfilling one of her purposes on earth, which was to serve others.

A KINDNESS CHECKLIST

- Rejoice for others' honorable, just, pure, lovely, and commendable actions.

- Forgive others for their mistakes and imperfections.

- Surround yourself with those who are in sync with your level of kindness. For example, those who have forgiving hearts, positive attitudes, walk in the fruits-of-the-Spirit behaviors, et cetera.

- Being kind does not mean ignoring your preferences and solely meeting others. However, being compromising at times is a kind gesture.

- Become conscious of others' definitions of kindness. If it is healthy for you, seek to treat them in that manner. For example, your mom may prefer a phone call from you regularly, and your coworker may prefer to drink their morning coffee before they communicate with others.

- Speak using gentle, kind words and tone when communicating, and strife will stay far away.

- Refrain from name-calling, blaming, yelling, or spiteful or jealous behaviors. If you find yourself experiencing these feelings, stop (unplug), move away from the target, evaluate why, forgive, and pray for a loving resolution.

Chapter Eighteen

THE FRUIT OF GOODNESS

*"Therefore, as we have opportunity, let us do good to all, especially to
those who are of the household of faith."*

GALATIANS 6:10

was homeless for a short period of time. Once I became financially
stable, I encountered others who were homeless. I offered to pay for
a few people's places to stay for a short period, while they accumulated
paychecks or cash to independently rent a room or get a roommate. God
rescued me out of hard times, so I gladly paid it forward.

Goodness includes being righteous and giving to others from your
heart without seeking a gain from your actions. Goodness can be provided
in a multitude of ways. Here is another example.

In the story Jesus told in Luke 10:35, it says, "On the next day, when
he departed, he took out two denarii, gave them to the innkeeper, and said
to him, 'Take care of him; and whatever more you spend, when I come
again, I will repay you.'"

The good Samaritan saw a man in need, and he interrupted his livelihood to help the stranger. This is an example of interrupting your life to put someone else before you. The generosity, kindness, and patience from the good Samaritan was priceless. Jesus came on earth and demonstrated at the highest level to put someone else's needs before your own.

At times, God approves for us to be called away from our own personal agenda to tend to others who are in need, such as going on mission trips to serve others, et cetera. Whoever you believe God would like for you to tend to their needs for a season, please consult God. Fast and pray to God before you make major decisions to take mission trips, take in a homeless person, rent a place for the less fortunate, et cetera. It took Daniel twenty-one days of fasting and praying before he heard from God's Holy Angels. So be patient, pray, fast, and wait for God's response.

God's goodness of fruits, vegetables, and nuts alone have a list of healthy blessings to combat pollution, toxicity, cancer cells, et cetera. God's antioxidants and multiple vitamins and nutrients within His creations help rid harmful things from our bodies while we are visitors on earth. That is extremely generous of God.

Remember, we are of God's image; therefore, we have multiple ways we can be *Good* toward others. Goodness from you could be to invest time doing research to share your knowledge with others of how many resources God has available for us on earth to aid humans. God has millions of things for us to righteously do. As we take an hour a day to *solely* praise and worship God for all His greatness and love, we open ourselves up to receive creative ideas, answers to questions we've been wondering, and a whole lot of positive thoughts we can use throughout our day to apply toward reaching our goals. We have learned how to do so many things with the resources God makes available to us and there are more gifts and ways to use God's generous blessings of this earth. Come on and get started with sharing them.

Christians strive to live a good and virtuous lifestyle. They courageously do the right thing the right way. They often go around edifying one another, complying with laws and policies, promoting peace as a peacemaker within the environment, donating some of their time, money, and resources to help others. They sincerely desire to help people. They are all-around good stewards. However, there are some good and virtuous Christians who long to provide some of their time, money, or resources to help others, but they find themselves always experiencing a setback within their own lives, making it difficult for them to donate their time, money, or resources to help people. There are plenty of reasons a Christian may constantly experience hardship. For example, there may be areas in their lives that either their bloodline or they, themselves, have not repented and settled a debt that is owed.

An example in the Bible is when Joshua had signed a treaty with the Gibeonites before consulting God and, as a result, was tricked into a peace (no killing) treaty with the Gibeonites. The agreement was binding. Later, Saul broke the peace treaty by killing some of the Gibeonites. This caused a curse, which came in the form of a famine. During the reign of David, there was a famine, time after time, because of Saul's sins. God explained to David the reason for the hardship, which legally came upon them because of Saul's sins. David went to the Gibeonites and asked what he could do to make amends. David was told, and approved, some of Saul's sons must die, which would end the famine curse. Praise God that our Lord and Savior, Jesus Christ, came and changed the way we make amends.

Jesus taught us how to settle conflict with love, repentance, and forgiveness, and not by an eye for an eye. However, curses on finances, health, family, relationships, et cetera, still exist. But the blood of Jesus Christ can cleanse us from strongholds and curses. If generation after generation, your family has struggled financially, pray to God for revelation on how to make amends lovingly and righteously. Stay committed to living a life that is walking in the fruits of the Spirit.

A GOOD STEWARD AND FINANCIAL ABUNDANCE

Plant good financial seeds. God loves for us to be cheerful givers. Although there are many ways that we can give without financially giving, it is very pleasing to God when we can give to the less fortunate without boasting.

"But when you do a charitable deed, do not let your left hand know what your right hand is doing, that your charitable deed may be in secret; and your Father who sees in secret will Himself reward you openly."

MATTHEW 6:3-4

When Christians are prosperous, Christians can help others in great ways. In 2 Corinthians 9:7, Paul talks about how God loves a cheerful giver: "So let each one give as he purposes in his heart, not grudgingly or of necessity; for God loves a cheerful giver."

Financial prosperity can bring upon a sense of financial peace in multiple areas of your life, giving you an opportunity to be a cheerful giver. Utilize some of your earnings to establish such a lifestyle.

This list is not an all-inclusive list to the road of financial prosperity, but it is just a few suggestions to get you started. Try doing the following:

- Create a savings account. Only use this account in emergencies, during slow money seasons, or for unforeseen expenses that may surface.

- Pay off debts.

- Create accounts for tithes and offerings.

- Purchase real estate.

- Maintain good credit.

- Maintain insurance coverage and allowance for repairs.

- Do not indulge in recklessly splurging on purchases with money. For example, avoid the gluttony of eating out, being a shopaholic, et cetera. Renounce such spirits and ask God for help to control such behaviors.

- Create multiple resources for money. These include stocks, 401K retirement plan, real estate, pensions (there a few companies who currently offer pensions), savings accounts, IRAs, et cetera.

TIPS ON WAYS TO BE A GOOD STEWARD WITH YOUR TIME

- Improve your environment, such as recycling and do not litter.

- Give recognition for kind gestures.

- Help someone complete one of their daily tasks.

- Teach children to give by donating their time to volunteer at an animal shelter, making inspirational cards to give to the sick, elderly, and less fortunate, giving "thank you" and birthday cards and videos to aunts, uncles, et cetera.

- Adopt an individual to pray for daily.

- Pray daily for missing children to be rescued. View some of their pictures and names, and pray they return home safely.

- Teach someone about Jesus' love. Win souls to Jesus Christ.

- Tell someone Jesus loves them.

- Discover and pray for someone to reach their personal goal.

TIPS ON WAYS TO BE A GOOD STEWARD MONETARILY

- Do something kind for a stranger at least once a month.

- Foster a pet and treat them to some goodies.

- Buy a family some groceries for a week.

- Discover family's and friends' goals. Do a one-time financial contribution toward their goals.

- Cash-app someone in need.

Chapter Nineteen

THE FRUIT OF FAITHFULNESS

"A faithful man will abound with blessings, but he who

hastens to be rich will not go unpunished."

PROVERBS 28:20

D eveloping a loving relationship with God, Jesus, the Holy Spirit, Holy Angels, family, friends, pets, and the self requires faithfulness. God provides us with a multitude of ways to experience faithfulness.

FAITHFUL TO THE KINGDOM OF GOD

Every day when we awake, we have a choice to walk in the fruits of the Spirit or not. We do so by choosing what thoughts, words, emotions, images, and actions in which we partake. Are we choosing the behaviors Jesus instructed for us? Act immediately when you awake. Start by reading the Bible, praying, and extending appreciation to God, Jesus Christ, the Holy Spirit, and the Holy Angels. Pray daily for billions of Holy Angels to be empowered with armor and strength to defeat and destroy Satan's schemes to hurt humans. Pray the Holy Angels guard Jesus Christ's followers and their families throughout each day, as well as potential souls who may give their lives over to become followers of Jesus Christ. Then, proceed throughout your day with love, joy, peace, patience, kindness, goodness, faithfulness, gentleness, and self-control.

If we do not develop habits to take time to serve the Kingdom of God and walk in the fruits of the Spirit daily, we put ourselves at risk for sin to be at our doors, awaiting to rule over us with strongholds, backsliding, oppression, et cetera.

FAITHFUL TO FAMILY

The book of Ruth illustrates how Ruth remained faithful to her mother-in-law Naomi, after Naomi's sons died, which included Ruth's husband. Ruth was young, had no children, and was free to return to her hometown and start a new life, but she chose to stay faithful in being part of a family with Naomi.

After Naomi's husband and sons died, Naomi was left with two daughters-in-law in a foreign land. She decided to return to Judah from Moab, where she had been living (Ruth 1:6-7). Because she cared for her daughters-in-law, she requested them to return to their own mothers' houses, explaining that she had no more sons to give (Ruth 1:8-13). But Ruth's heart toward Naomi and her desire to become a worshiper of God caused Ruth to boldly embrace the unknown with Naomi (Ruth 1:14-17).

Naomi had wanted what she believed would be the best choice for Ruth.

But Ruth replied, "'Entreat me not to leave you, *or to* turn back from following after you; for wherever you go, I will go; and wherever you lodge, I will lodge; your people *shall be* my people, and your God, my God,'" (Ruth 1:16).

Naomi's other daughter-in-law returned to her hometown, while Ruth bravely went to Naomi's hometown to build a life with her, ready to conquer many challenges. God blessed Ruth with a husband and a child to add to her family.

At times, with balance, faithfulness may require us to temporarily put others' needs before our own. Ruth staying committed to taking care of what was left of her family—which was Naomi—instead of returning to her own town, was a high level of selflessness and faithfulness.

A MOTHER'S FAITHFULNESS

"I wish I was not in this family!" said nine-year-old William to his mother.

William was upset. He could not play basketball with his friends that afternoon because he had homework. While he was walking to his room, looking defeated, William's mother Collette requested him to have a seat. She talked with him about saying hurtful words to her and the importance of staying faithful to his obligations, even when he'd rather be doing something else. He hugged his mom and apologized. Collette forgave him and advised him on healthier ways to release his frustration. William went into his room to finish his homework. She went to cook his dinner and iron his school clothes.

Collette's loving heart allowed her to maintain faithfulness in her role as a loving parent to her son, even when his mistakes hurt her. When someone continuously reinforces meeting our expectations, it motivates us to be faithful with them. William grew up experiencing his mother Collette being faithful in overseeing him staying committed to his education and other responsibilities. Years later, William received a scholarship and achieved graduating with a bachelor's degree. Being faithful can prevent unnecessary delays in accomplishing our goals and dreams. Had William not stayed faithful in doing his work, the opportunities for college scholarships may not have been offered, nor the opportunity to attend a prestigious college immediately after high school. Maintain faithfulness through righteous commitment.

Maintaining faith in God and appreciating His faithfulness every day can inspire us to be faithful within our relationships.

DANIEL'S FAITHFULNESS

Praying with a heart full of love and faith is a sure way to accelerate your prayers to Heaven. In Daniel 10, Daniel was filled with great sorrow when he prayed to God about a troubling vision. Daniel was in anguish for twenty-one days. Although his prayers were immediately heard, he did not receive an immediate response, because the Holy Angel had to fight Satanic forces and call upon the powerful Holy Angel Michael to assist in overpowering Satan's forces to reach Daniel and communicate the answers to his prayer request. The Holy Angels had to go through a Satanic territorial area to reach him.

Like Daniel, sometimes situations happen, and we find ourselves oppressed to the point where we cannot get out of the situation without the supernatural help of God. You may not get an immediate answer from Heaven, but hang in there. God's Holy Angels may be fighting to get answers to you. Your job is to keep your mind and heart on loving God, yourself, and others, and away from sin. Rest assured that the energy from your loving heart and soul is traveling your request to Heaven. So, stay faithful in praying and being obedient to Jesus' instruction, which is to walk in love.

It was twenty-four days before Daniel received an answer and he was steadfast in praying and fasting. So, it may take some time. However, keep in mind, if you have stored unforgiveness, hate, jealousy, et cetera, I can assure you the energy from an unrepentant, unforgiving, and unloving heart will not be as effective as the prayers of a repenting and forgiving heart. When we follow God's instructions, our energy maintains a loving vibration. To do so, keep praying and believing in God for deliverance.

Many times, when we are waiting for an answer or healing, there is a huge spiritual fight ongoing between the Kingdom of God and Satan's demons. The demonic forces may be trying to distract you from praying and convince you to give up on your faith, while at the same time, your Holy Angel is sending you encouragement to keep the faith and keep praying. Because help *is* on the way. Do not give up and be subdued by Satan's distractions. Remember, it took twenty-four days before Daniel got edification.

FAITH IN JESUS

"Let not your heart be troubled; you believe in God, believe also in Me. In My Father's house are many mansions; if it were not so, I would have told you. I go to prepare a place for you. And if I go and prepare a place for you, I will come again and receive you to Myself; that where I am, there you may be also. And where I go you know, and the way you know.' Thomas said to Him, 'Lord, we do not know where You are going, and how can we know the way?' Jesus said to him, 'I am the way, the truth, and the life. No one comes to the Father except through Me. If you had known Me, you would have known My Father also; and from now on you know Him and have seen Him.' Philip said to Him, 'Lord, show us the Father, and it is sufficient for us.' Jesus said to him, "Have I been with you so long, and yet you have not known Me, Philip? He who has seen Me has seen the Father; so how can you say, "Show us the Father"? Do you not believe that I am in the Father, and the Father in Me? The

words that I speak to you I do not speak on My own authority; but the Father who

dwells in Me does the works. Believe Me that I am in the Father and the Father in

Me, or else believe Me for the sake of the works themselves.'"

JOHN 14:1-11

The greater your faith is in Jesus and in adhering to His instructions to turn away from sin and walk in love, the more empowered you become. Out of love, Jesus died on the cross for our sins. Out of love for Jesus, I feel compelled to turn away from sin and walk in the fruits of the Spirit. A multitude of sins is covered as we strive to walk in the fruits of the Spirit (which is walking in love) instead of walking in the flesh, where one is subject to sin.

REMAINING FAITHFUL TO YOUR GOALS

Opportunity comes within our lives to manifest our dreams when we faithfully speak, think, imagine, believe, and work hard on our dreams. Daniel and Collette's son, William, is a testimony of how sowing faithfulness reaps rewards.

To maintain being faithful with your current responsibilities and simultaneously working on your dreams is wise. Take time in the present to work as if your dreams are already here. If you aspire to be a physical trainer, but you are working for a fast-food chain, give yourself some extra time each day to work on your dream. Complete courses that will aid you in developing your skills. Maintain meeting your current employer's expectations, while feeling excited to return home to work toward your goals. Apply the thoughts, words, and belief, and imagine that you are currently a physical trainer. Do work each day to achieve your certification as a physical trainer, such as spending a few minutes performing in the mirror to feel as if you are currently training clients. This will fuel your energy and motivation. Volunteer as a trainer. Give family and friends free classes to build a resume and a clientele base. Seek a mentor and stay in the present moment, so you can recognize when opportunities surface to obtain a physical trainer position.

The energy from your thoughts, words, belief, images, and work will manifest opportunities for you. Be ready!

WAYS TO BE FAITHFUL

- Keep your eyes on God by memorizing scriptures of God's promises and meditating on them daily.

- Frequently check your state of emotions to ensure you stay away from fear and doubt of God's promises. If you find yourself getting discouraged, open the Bible and read the story of God keeping His promise to Abraham (Genesis 17:1-17).

- Pray to God for guidance about your decisions and options before you commit to someone.

- Be honest. Do not fear telling someone no if you are not able to fulfill their requests. It is much better to be honest, instead of getting involved in an obligation you later will not be able to fulfill. It will also provide that person time to pursue someone else, who may be qualified to accept the commitment.

- Stay inspired by maintaining an awareness that your obligations within relationships positively impact others. You matter. Your actions matter.

- Maintain faithfulness in exercising the fruits-of-the-Spirit behaviors, so God's love energy can move God's promises within your life. God is always faithful.

- Maintain faithfulness toward your existing responsibilities before you take on other responsibilities.

- Pray and ask the Holy Spirit and Holy Angels to help you be faithful.

Chapter Twenty

THE FRUIT OF GENTLENESS

*"But we were gentle among you, just as a nursing
mother cherishes her own children."*

1 THESSALONIANS 2:7

In John 13, Jesus washes His disciples' feet, which teaches us that we should gladly serve one another with humble and gentle hearts. Regardless of our powers, titles, or social statuses, we are to be humble and gentle. Jesus instructs us to be humble. Jesus, who has all power, humbled Himself to those who needed Him, and Jesus needed absolutely nothing from them.

Do you speak gently to the people who may not have anything to offer you, such as children, animals, the elderly, or other vulnerable people? Do you treat those whom you need, or those who have more than you, the same as those whom have less than you?

Tenderness and calmness are often applied when one is being gentle with others.

COMMUNICATE WITH GENTLENESS

A friend named Keith presented Lynn a proposal that was greatly beneficial for him with hardly any benefits for her. Had she accepted the offer, it could have set her back atrociously. She was offended by the lack of consideration for her, more so because she thought of him as a friend who cared about her well-being. The more she thought about his offer, the angrier she became. But at the same time, she wanted to maintain calmness as she declined his offer. She was too angry to deliver an immediate, yet gentle response, even though she had an immediate answer. So she decided to be patient and renew her thoughts and emotions to a state of gentleness. She proceeded with her daily routines and tried to avoid any more thoughts of him to calm herself down.

Later that day, the thoughts of him resurfaced and she got terribly angry again. She prayed and asked in Jesus' name with the power of the Holy Spirit to help her release anger and forgive Keith. She thought of all the times she repented to God, and God always forgave. She thought about the times she had done something that was maybe not fair to others; however, they continued to show love. Thoughts continued to resurface on how her self-absorbed actions in the past had caused her to be unfair to others. This revelation opened her heart to feel humility. To feel forgiveness toward Keith.

So, the next day, she was ready to reply with gentleness. Here is a similar response she provided him:

Dear Keith,

I am not able to accept your offer, because your compensation for the work, time, and resources I am required to provide is under budget for me to pay my staff. To reconsider, this offer would require the following allowance and resources to be included . . .

Had she not calmed down before her reply, her response would not have been gentle; instead, it would have possibly been hurtful, destroying his image of her as the go-to Christian for advice and prayers.

If someone is angry with you, how do you prefer them to communicate with you? Would you like for them to talk in private and with a calm voice, sharing how they feel and asking questions? Most people prefer a gentle delivery of constructive feedback, instead of yelling and accusing you.

Gentle energy comes out naturally from a gentle heart. Choose a gentle tone, words, emotions, and kind thoughts. Exclude yelling, screaming, blaming, and name-calling from your conversation. Do not force people to interact with you. Surround yourself with those who aim for restoration, comfort one another, and righteously agree with one another. Remember to unplug when you feel yourself doing unkind behaviors and plug in (to be in the present moment) by choosing to view and appreciate things around you that come from God's generosity. Gentleness helps us to communicate constructively to everyday challenges with peace and love. It also helps the other person to not feel like they must flee or defend themselves. When challenges arise, such as accidently getting too close to someone inside the grocery store and almost hitting them, a gentle apology is appropriate. In your daily conversations, practice using a gentle tone and words such as *thank you, okay, I understand, I forgive you, unfortunately I will not be able to, it's okay, no one is perfect,* instead of saying harsh words such as *what do you want, that was dumb, hurry up, no, shut up.*

A GENTLENESS CHECKLIST

- Change your emotion to one of calmness before you speak.
- What are gentle words to you? Do you extend the same words in all your encounters?
- Talk low when feeling unpleasant emotions, as this will help to soften your voice.
- Kindly serve others often.
- Let go of pride and humble your words and tone to be gentle.

Chapter Twenty-One

THE FRUIT OF SELF-CONTROL

"I can do all things through Christ who strengthens me."

PHILIPPIANS 4:13

T wenty-two-year-old Joni took her four-year-old niece to the
bakery. Her niece chose a vanilla cupcake with rich, pink icing. As
they left the bakery and got in the car, Joni instructed her niece to wait
until she arrived home to eat some of her cupcake. Although her four-
year-old niece normally obeyed Joni, I guess the temptation was too great.
Needless to say, a few minutes into the drive, Joni's niece was giggling
in her car seat, holding her cupcake that she had taken a big chunk out,
having eaten a lot of the sugary icing. Joni looked at her with horror. Joni
said, "You will get sick from eating all that icing."

Joni reached and took the cupcake from her. By the time they arrived
home, which was thirty minutes later, her niece was slumped down in her
car seat and complaining her stomach was aching. Later that evening, her
stomach had calmed down and she looked at the box her cupcake was

in and frowned, saying, "I don't want that anymore. It made my tummy hurt."

At four years old, she could identify what caused her pain and was able to disassociate herself. How many of us can exercise self-control once we identify something will ultimately hurt us? A lot of times, sin initially starts out by providing us with a sensational feeling, like Joni's niece felt, but ultimately it will cause harm.

A great way to maintain self-control is to regularly fast to deny flesh desires and replace those desires with nourishment for our spirits, such as:

- Praise and worship God.

- Pray.

- Ask the Holy Spirit and Holy Angels for help.

- Read the Bible.

- Witness to others with John 3:16.

- Renounce demons.

- Replace your sin with a loving act.

- Repent and forgive.

- Walk in faith within all encounters.

CONTROLLING THE FLESH AND EMPOWERING THE SPIRIT

God's gift of love and power can be applied to rule over sin.

God generously provides time and mercy for the soul to unveil His truth. One reason is because God is so loving, patient, kind, and faithful. God is very aware that Satan and his demons currently roam the earth, tricking people by sending them deceitful thoughts and feelings. One of Satan's deceits is to trick people into believing Satan, demons, and Hell are not real. Satan sends thoughts and feelings that immoral sex, unforgiveness, and similar sins are okay. Just like he told Eve it was okay to do the forbidden. At times, souls seek the rationale and justification to do forbidden sins. Satan is right there to add to the soul's sinful thoughts and instigate the soul to sin. The soul then takes the bait.

The soul's spirit is working hard to warn the soul not to succumb to the enslavement of sin. A soul may ignore their spirit warning them to resist the sin because the sin feels good. What the sinful soul fails to realize is that each time he or she succumbs to sexual immorality, sensuality, idolatry, sorcery, enmity, strife, jealousy, fits of anger, rivalries, dissensions, divisions, envy, drunkenness, orgies, and similar behaviors, Satan is legally allowed to strap spiritual bondages of that sin onto the soul, making it feel extremely hard to walk away from the sin. The sinner often becomes angry if someone tries to come between them and their sin. Sometimes, the sinner has to experience the repeated loss of relationships, money, health, happiness, homelessness, et cetera, before they become humble enough to seek a way out of sin enslavement. I am not saying all hardship stems from a soul's sin. Other reasons can cause hardship. Spread the word to all souls who are being ruled by sin that in the name of our Lord and Savior, Jesus Christ, they can pray to God to get out of the bondages of sin.

I traveled along multiple paths to learn how to rule over sin and the most successful road for me was turning my attention from sin and toward learning how to love. Love. Love. Love. Love. And love in all areas of my life. I failed many times and had setbacks, but as I got up and forgave myself, forgave others, and pursued love, God began to fill my heart with an abundance of love and compassion for humans and animals, far more than I previously possessed. I had always wanted the best for people and now it was even greater.

I will never be perfect. I will never be completely without sin, but with God's allowance through Jesus Christ, our Lord and Savior, and by the strength and the power of the Holy Spirit and Holy Angels, I will consistently strive to forgive, repent, rule over sin, and show love toward God's creations.

If there is a strong dependency and desire for something outside of you to influence the inside of you to feel better, ask God for the motivation and strength to release the dependency and do the following:

- Ask God's permission for His Kingdom assistance to break the bondage.

- Thank God for everyone He allows to help you.

- Call upon God, Jesus, the Holy Spirit, and Holy Angels to heal and strengthen you.

- Plea the blood of Jesus, from the crown of your head to the soles of your feet. Repeat daily.

- Renounce demons from your body and relationships. Repeat daily.

- Pray and fast (if doctor approved).

- Forgive all whom you may hold an offense against within your heart.

WAYS TO MAINTAIN SELF-CONTROL

Believe you are healed. Thank God throughout the day for healing you. Remain humble toward God, Jesus, the Holy Spirit, and Holy Angels. Pray and give thanks daily for all their assistance.

Do the opposite of the things for which you may lack self-control. For example, if you have a talebearer spirit that tempts you to waste a lot of time viewing gossip sites and reality shows and spreading hurtful rumors, then do the opposite of your temptation, such as spreading the gospel, memorizing scriptures, watching Christian movies, reading the Bible, praying for others, et cetera. Divert your attention to do a kind gesture, such as wash, dry, and fold your relative's clothes.

Build up your physical energy as much as possible. Examples include exercise, proper sleep, eating healthy, et cetera. It's challenging to have self-control in facing temptation when the physical body is fragile and weak. Apply fifteen minutes each day toward your new, healthy habit to eventually replace your harmful habit. Nourish the physical, spiritual, and mental parts of you every day. When exercising and eating healthy, start slow, and gradually increase.

Extend godly love toward your thoughts, words, emotions, images, actions, sight, hearing, taste, touch, and smell. Energy from your loving behaviors will strengthen you.

Create images of Jesus casting the harmful habit from you. Believe the addiction or stronghold has been removed.

Remain in the present moment as much as possible and do positive things that cause you happiness. Stay plugged in to the present. Appreciate what you see, taste, feel, hear, and smell as much as possible and heighten your thoughts to create more or better feelings. In other words, if you want new marble floors, view your current wood floors and then imagine, with excitement and belief, that your floors are marble.

Recite this scripture: "What is impossible with man is possible with God," (Luke 18:27 ESV). Pray and read uplifting scriptures regarding having faith, courage, et cetera.

Chapter Twenty-Two

GLORIFY OUR LORD JESUS CHRIST

"For God so loved the world that He gave His only begotten Son, that whoever believes in Him should not perish but have everlasting life."

JOHN 3:16

An important expectation God has for us is for our hearts and minds, without a doubt, to believe that Jesus Christ taught mankind how to turn from sin and turn toward love, died for our salvation, and was resurrected three days later. Every day give thanks to Jesus for your healing from illnesses and curses, and for your salvation. Worship and praise Jesus every morning, throughout the day, and before you go to sleep.

Below is a list of the miraculous and extraordinary works of our Lord and Savior, Jesus Christ. Ask yourself, "Do I believe?" If the heart is not convinced, pray to God to renew your heart and mind to understand, believe, and trust in Jesus. Renounce any demon that may be trying to interfere. Believe in Jesus. Invite Jesus' healing power into your life.

SOME OF THE MIRACLES JESUS PERFORMED

1. Jesus restored a shriveled hand (Matthew 12:10-13).

2. Jesus cured a possessed man (Matthew 12:22).

3. Jesus fed at least five thousand people (Matthew 14:15-21).

4. Jesus cured a woman (Matthew 15:22-28).

5. Jesus healed a deaf man (Mark 7:31-37).

6. Jesus healed a blind man (Mark 8:22-26).

7. Jesus cured a boy who was plagued by a demon (Matthew 17:14-21).

8. Jesus cured a man of dropsy (Luke 14:1-4).

9. Jesus cleansed lepers (Luke 17:11-17).

10. Jesus raised Lazarus from the dead (John 11:1-44).

11. Jesus caused the fig tree to wither (Matthew 21:18-22).

12. Jesus restored the ear of the high priest's servant (Luke 22:50-51).

13. Jesus brought about the second great haul of fishes (John 21:1-14).

14. Jesus changed water into wine (John 2:1-11).

15. Jesus cured the nobleman's son (John 4:46-51).

16. Jesus cast out an unclean spirit (Mark 1:23-28).

17. Jesus cured Simon's mother-in-law of a fever (Mark 1:30-31).

18. Jesus healed the centurion's servant (Matthew 8:5-13).

19. Jesus raised the widow's son from the dead (Luke 7:11-18).

20. Jesus calmed the storm (Mark 4:35-39).

21. Jesus raised the ruler's daughter from the dead (Matthew 9:18-26).

22. Jesus cured a woman of an issue of blood (Luke 8:43-48).

23. Jesus loosened the tongue of a man who could not speak (Matthew 9:32-33).

ACKNOWLEDGMENTS

I would like to express a deep appreciation and indebtedness to the following: My Heavenly Father, Lord, and Savior Jesus Christ; Holy Spirit; and Holy Angels. Special thanks to the following: My late parents Aaron and Delores Hill; my daughter, Brittany Pressley; my nephew Rodney Richards; and my family, friends, business associates, and others for helping me in one way or another.

SCRIPTURES TO EMPOWER A LIFESTYLE OF GOD'S LOVE

Memorize a verse of scripture daily. Scriptures can inspire believers to build a strong relationship with God and live a lifestyle full of God's love.

GOD EXPECTS US TO LOVE

"'And you shall love the Lord your God with all your heart, with all your soul, with all your mind, and with all your strength.' This *is* the first commandment." (Mark 12:30)

"Beloved, let us love one another, for love is of God; and everyone who loves is born of God and knows God." (1 John 4:7)

"He who does not love does not know God, for God is love." (1 John 4:8)

"Let all *that* you *do* be done with love." (1 Corinthians 16:14)

"Therefore you shall love the Lord your God, and keep His charge, His statutes, His judgments, and His commandments always." (Deuteronomy 11:1)

"Therefore love the stranger, for you were strangers in the land of Egypt." (Deuteronomy 10:19)

BUILDING A RELATIONSHIP WITH THE KINGDOM OF GOD

"If you abide in Me, and My words abide in you, you will ask what you desire, and it shall be done for you." (John 15:7)

"Also it shall be, when he sits on the throne of his kingdom, that he shall write for himself a copy of this law in a book, from the one before the priests, the Levites. And it shall be with him, and he shall read it all the days of his life, that he may learn to fear the Lord his God and be careful to observe all the words of this law and these statutes." (Deuteronomy 17:18-19)

"Now I rejoice, not that you were made sorry, but that your sorrow led to repentance. For you were made sorry in a godly manner, that you might suffer loss from us in nothing." (2 Corinthians 7:9)

"And those who *are* Christ's have crucified the flesh with its passions and desires." (Galatians 5:24)

"By this we know that we abide in Him, and He in us, because He has given us of His Spirit." (1 John 4:13)

"Set your mind on things above, not on things on the earth." (Colossians 3:2)

"For the flesh lusts against the Spirit, and the Spirit against the flesh; and these are contrary to one another, so that you do not do the things that you wish." (Galatians 5:17)

"But if you are led by the Spirit, you are not under the law." (Galatians 5:18)

"Then Peter said to them, 'Repent, and let every one of you be baptized in the name of Jesus Christ for the remission of sins; and you shall receive the gift of the Holy Spirit." (Acts 2:38)

"But the Helper, the Holy Spirit, whom the Father will send in My name, He will teach you all things, and bring to your remembrance all things that I said to you." (John 14:26)

"I say then: Walk in the Spirit, and you shall not fulfill the lust of the flesh." (Galatians 5:16)

"And do not be drunk with wine, in which is dissipation; but be filled with the Spirit." (Ephesian 5:18)

"But you are not in the flesh but in the Spirit, if indeed the Spirit of God dwells in you. Now if anyone does not have the Spirit of Christ, he is not His." (Romans 8:9)

"Or do you not know that your body is the temple of the Holy Spirit who is in you, whom you have from God, and you are not your own?" (1 Corinthians 6:19)

"Now may the God of hope fill you with all joy and peace in believing, that you may abound in hope by the power of the Holy Spirit." (Romans 15:13)

LOVING BEHAVIORS AND NON-LOVING (SIN) BEHAVIORS

"But the fruit of the Spirit is love, joy, peace, longsuffering, kindness, goodness, faithfulness, gentleness, self-control. Against such there is no law." (Galatians 5:22-23)

"Now the works of the flesh are evident, which are: adultery, fornication, uncleanness, lewdness, idolatry, sorcery, hatred, contentions, jealousies, outbursts of wrath, selfish ambitions, dissensions, heresies, envy, murders, drunkenness, revelries, and the like; of which I tell you beforehand, just as I told *you* in past time, that those who practice such things will not inherit the kingdom of God." (Galatians 5:19-21)

MEMORIZE THESE SCRIPTURES TO INSPIRE YOU

As soon as you feel a tad bit of anxiety, fear, anger, doubt, et cetera, immediately say numerous times the below scriptures that are relevant to how you are feeling in that moment. Renounce the demons associated with the negative emotions.

For **Courage** when your feel fear:
"Finally, my brethren, be strong in the Lord and in the power of His might." (Ephesians 6:10)

For **Forgiveness** when you feel resentment:
"Judge not, and you shall not be judged. Condemn not, and you shall not be condemned. Forgive, and you will be forgiven." (Luke 6:37)

For **Love** when you feel brokenhearted:
"And above all things have fervent love for one another, for 'love will cover a multitude of sins.'" (1 Peter 4:8)

For **Faith** when you feel doubt:
"You will keep *him* in perfect peace, whose mind *is* stayed *on You,* because he trusts in You." (Isaiah 26:3)

For **Hope** when you feel defeated:
"For he who sows to his flesh will of the flesh reap corruption, but he who sows to the Spirit will of the Spirit reap everlasting life." (Galatians 6:8)

For **Patience** when you feel impatient:
"With all lowliness and gentleness, with longsuffering, bearing with one another in love." (Ephesians 4:2)

For **Strength** when you feel weak:
"But the Lord is faithful, who will establish you and guard *you* from the evil one." (2 Thessalonians 3:3)

GLOSSARY OF TERMS

3rd Heaven: Paradise. The glorious residence of God's Kingdom, which includes the Father, the Son, the Holy Spirit, and Holy Angels. This place is beyond human sight.

Born-Again Christian: A sinner who has repented of their sins; believes and accepts Jesus Christ as their Lord and Savior; and, as a result, their spirit is reborn and they become a part of God's family.

Energy Holes and Cracks: This is when the body covering has been impaired and is in need of being restored, making one susceptible to low vibration encounters.

Equally Yoked: To share and practice with balance the same level of belief system.

God: The Father of Jesus Christ. Creator of all. The only Ruler, the King of kings, and Lord of lords, who alone is immortal and who lives in unapproachable light, of whom no living human has seen or can see. To him be honor and glory forever.

High Vibration: An environment where loving behaviors are being reciprocated, such as the fruits of the Spirit, impacting a person with such a heart and mind to often experience loving encounters. It's an environment where Holy Angels often tread.

Holy Angels: Holy Angels ward off demons, and they protect the believers and unbelievers from harm. Holy Angels communicate our needs to God, motivate us, and more.

Holy Spirit: The Holy Spirit, abides in the believers of Jesus Christ and is able to bring peace beyond understanding to the believer. The Holy Spirit is the spirit of God within the lives of believers. Demons fear the Holy Spirit. The Holy Spirit brings upon healing to the believer. The Holy Spirit is a source of truth, intelligence, miracles, and power.

Jesus: The son of God. He was both God and man. Jesus was sent by God to save mankind from sin that was inherited through the Fall of Adam.

Low Vibration: An environment of non-loving behaviors, such as jealousy, hatred, fear, greed, alcoholism, depression, and similar behaviors. It is an environment where demons rule. A person's body covering may experience holes and be highly susceptible to problems.

Redemption (Salvation): A gift from God to save a sinner, who chooses to become a born-again Christian through Jesus Christ's sacrificial death for humans' sins.

Spiritual World: The environment of those who do not have physical bodies, such as spirits and Angels.

CPSIA information can be obtained
at www.ICGtesting.com
Printed in the USA
LVHW050442011021
699185LV00003B/44